RICHARD A. HARDIN

MERCY GRACE CHARITY

GOD'S LOVE TO MANKIND

MERCY GRACE CHARITY by Richard A. Hardin
ISBN: 1453806962 EAN-13: 9781453806968

All scripture quotes are taken from the King James Version, Cambridge, 1769.

DEDICATION

"Mercy, Grace, Charity" is dedicated to the Spirit of Grace who has been for years and is still being falsely misrepresented as "God's unmerited favor" by the majority of Christian ministers in our society. As great as God's unmerited favor, mercy, is to unrepentant sinners who God blesses to draw to repentance, Romans 2:4, this misrepresentation of the Spirit of Grace has been used by the devil to cause much confusion about the wonderful grace of God that transforms sinners hearts and engrafts them into the family of God. The devil will do anything he can to degrade the grace of God because grace is the fruit of Jesus' righteousness that He saw with joy beyond the sufferings of the cross so He willingly submitted Himself for us to the torture of the cross to become the foundation or means of our forgiveness of sin and transformation into the family of God. Grace is the work of the Spirit of God in mankind's hearts for salvation and after salvation to help us grow to be like Jesus.

THANKS

I want to express my thanks to my son, Dwain Hardin, DNA Graphics, for the beautiful design and layout of my book and cover.

TABLE of CONTENTS

INTRODUCTION

God in His beauty reflected by His creation has come to mankind in many ways, methods or means, to try to draw mankind back into fellowship with Him as stated by the Apostle Paul in *Romans 1:19-20, "Because that which may be known of God is manifest in them; for 'God hath shewed it unto them.' (20) For the invisible things of Him from the creation of the world are clearly seen, being understood by the things that are made, even His eternal power and Godhead; so that they are without excuse."* Scripturally there is no such thing as an atheist, only unbelievers who have willfully rejected God when He revealed Himself to them. When God manifests Himself to us in a way that we recognize His presence, we often say, "God spoke to us, or God sent His love to us," when in reality God is not sending anything to us; it is God Himself coming to us because God is Love; therefore, it would be impossible for God to separate Himself from Love and send Love to us, *1 John 4:8, 16, "He hat loveth not knoweth not God: for God is love. (16) And we have known and believed the love that God hath to us. God is love; and he that dwelleth in love dwelleth in God, and God in him."* The manifestation of God to us from His Spirit to and through our physical senses of smelling, seeing, hearing, feeling and tasting is called or referred to as our "hearing God," through the third part of the Trinity, Christ the Living Word or Holy Spirit.

When we receive the Spirit of Christ into our hearts and become new creatures in Christ, we each are faced with certain responsibilities as shown in

2 Corinthians 5:17-20, "Therefore if any man be in Christ, he is a new creature: old things are passed away; behold, all things are become new. (18) And all things are of God, who hath reconciled us to Himself by Jesus Christ, and hath given to us the ministry of reconciliation; (19) To wit, that God was in Christ, reconciling the world unto Himself, not imputing their trespasses unto them; and hath committed unto us the Word of Reconciliation. (20) Now then we are ambassadors for Christ, as though God did beseech you by us: we pray you in Christ's stead, be ye reconciled to God." In our Ministry of Reconciliation, as ambassadors for Christ, we each should be seeking to share the pure Words of Reconciliation to others. When we share the pure Words of Reconciliation, it is the Living Word or Christ in and through us that we will be speaking to others, or God speaking through us and those Words we speak will go forth with the full power and wisdom of the Creator Living Word, Christ. God will back up His Word through His people if we speak it accurately as the Lord stated by the prophet Isaiah in *Isaiah 44:28, "(God) That confirmeth the word of His servant, and performeth the counsel of His messengers."* In *2 Kings 20:1-11*, God moved the earth and sun to confirm His Word that Isaiah spoke to King Hezekiah, and God even backed up His Word through the donkey to Balaam in Numbers Chapter 22. God will back up His Word through us if we speak His Word pure without change, but if we change the words by adding to or taking away from the Words of Reconciliation then we will be speaking our words, not the Living Word, Christ, and God will not back up what we say as stated in *Proverbs 30:5-6, "Every Word of God is pure: He is a shield unto them that put their trust in Him. (6) Add thou not unto His Words,(Christ), lest He reprove thee, and thou be found a liar."* In *Psalms 138:2,* God's Pure Word is magnified above all of God's names because God's Pure Word is Christ, the Living Word! In our witnessing, preaching, or teaching, we must be very careful to speak God's Word correctly because satan is doing everything he can on both ends of our conversations to ruin or block our communication of God's pure message of His Love for and to mankind. We must try to be as accurate, clear, and as specific as we can when we share the Words of Reconciliation because they are the gospel of our Lord Jesus Christ. Jesus speaks of our need to be con*cerned about our words in Matthew 12:36-37, "But I say unto you, That ever idle word that men shall speak, they shall give account thereof in the day of judgment. (37) For by thy words thou shalt be justified, and by thy words thou shalt be condemned."* Even today many of our idle words may be keeping some of our loved ones and friends from receiving our testimony of Christ because God is not able to speak His Spirit, Christ, or the Pure Word through us to them as He desires. In our Bible studies as Christians, we should make it a top priority to study the Scriptures to be able to share the true, pure words of salvation, *Proverbs 11:30 states, "The fruit of the righteous is a tree of life; and he that winneth souls is wise,"* and *Daniel 12:3 states, "And they that be wise shall shine as the brightness of the firmament; and they that turn many to righteousness as the stars forever and ever."* Our primary goal should be to witness or be available daily to witness to each person we meet and to give an accurate, clear, specific testimony of the requirements for salvation through the Lord Jesus Christ.

In trying to communicate a message, we are trying to take an idea or picture from our mind and describe it verbally or in writing so that anyone listening to or reading the material will receive the same idea or picture in their minds. The main reason we should be accurate and speak God's Pure Word is that while we are speaking to the ears of a person, and we are speaking God's Pure Word, then His Living Word, Christ, will be speaking at the same time to the person's heart while we are speaking to the person's head. God will be working with us if we speak His Pure Word, but if we have added idle words then as in *Proverbs 30:5-6,* given above, He will not back up what we say for it will be our powerless words, not His.

In every area of study that I can remember since my first grade in school, there seems to have been the pattern of a brief introduction to the new material and then immediately a study of the meanings or definitions of some of the new unique words we would need to be able to understand the new material. The foundational words for every area of study are very important, for we cannot progress to the deeper important concepts if we do not understand the basics whether it is in math, law, nuclear physics, or Christianity. Even with all of the efforts to standardize definitions in every field of endeavor, ineffective communication is still one of the greatest problems causing conflict, mistakes, and sometimes even death. Married couples, employees, or other closely related people will often fuss and verbally fight for some time and then one will say, **"Well, I thought you meant ..."** and the other will then reply, **"I thought you were saying..."** Clear, specific communications is beneficial in every area of our lives. In Christianity incorrect, vague, or communications filled with levity could be worse than deadly; for some of the listeners, confusion in our messages could result in their having to live an eternal life of torment in the Lake of Fire. The stakes are high, and often we only have one opportunity to share with people we meet in the marketplace. The Apostle Peter encourages us to always be ready and willing to share the reason for our hope of Christ in *1 Peter 3:15, "But sanctify the Lord God in your hearts: and be ready always to give an answer to every man that asketh you a reason of the hope that is in you with meekness and fear."* Jesus explains about sanctification in

John 17:17 when He states in His prayer, *"Sanctify them through thy truth: thy Word is truth."* The Apostle Peter is encouraging us to sanctify our hearts or to fill our hearts with the Living Word, Christ, and be ready to share the Word with anyone who asks or who will allow us to share with them, and we should share our message accurately with meekness fearing the person might reject if we are in anyway abrasive or confusing.

When we try to communicate an accurate, clear, specific message to another person we must be very concerned about how we present the material because there are so many hindrances to effective communications: misspelled or mispronounced words, multiple meanings to words, incorrect word usage, incorrect punctuation, various moods of those who receive the message, unintentional offensive terms in the message, and especially for Christian messages, the various beliefs of those receiving the message. A message about salvation which includes some of these mistakes might sound very thrilling and uplifting to some but not have the clear understandable information to develop a proper image or procedure in other listeners' minds as to what they should specifically do to receive salvation.

I have heard it said in Bible studies and radio and television messages that faith and trust are basically interchangeable, but they are very different. Trust is based on a relationship of confidence in something or someone, and faith only comes from hearing, accepting, and obeying God's specific Pure Word. The difference is shown in, "Do you trust God enough to believe that He will strengthen and help you so that you have the courage to accept His Words and obey when He asks you to teach the Sunday School class even though you do not feel qualified?" Doubt and unbelief are often used interchangeably and are both undesirable but also very different; doubt is a head problem when we do not know God's Will, and unbelief is a heart problem when we know His will but do not love Him enough to obey His Will. Many Christians have rejected God's call to teach classes, to work with the youth or elderly, to preach or other callings to service, and they do not realize that even as Christians they are living in unbelief and have given satan advantage in their lives. It is evidenced by many Christians who live with visible curses of sicknesses that are listed in *Deuteronomy Chapter 28*. The Apostle Paul states in 2 Corinthians 2:10-11 that we must forgive others or we will give satan the advantage in our life, and this applies to willfully rejecting any of God's Word to service. We Christians will have to answer for rejecting these callings when we stand before the judgment seat of Christ, *2 Corinthians 5:10, "For we must all appear before the Judgment seat of Christ; that every one may receive the things done in his body, according to that he hath done, whether it be good or bad."*

God does not require that we know all of the specifics of the "Christian" words to become "saved," "Born Again," or one of His Children; all we must do is call out to Him from a repentant heart asking His forgiveness and committing our life to Him as shown in *2 Corinthians 3:16, "Nevertheless when it (the heart) shall turn to the Lord, the vail shall be taken away."* God hears heart language, and when a heart turns to God, the vail of separation between God and man is removed regardless of the audible language used. The audible language might only be a cry of **"God,"** or **"Help,"** but coming from a repentant heart, God will hear and respond. After we receive the Spirit of His Son into our hearts at salvation and start growing in knowledge and understanding of God and His ways, God expects us as His ambassadors to represent Him faithfully with accuracy, *2 Corinthians 5:20, "Now then we are ambassadors for Christ,* *as though God did beseech you by us: we pray you in Christ's stead, be ye reconciled to God."* He will only back up His Pure Word as stated again in *Proverbs 30:5-6, "Every Word of God is Pure: He is a shield unto them that put their trust in Him. (6) Add thou not unto His Words, lest He reprove thee, and thou be found a liar."* An ambassador must share the pure word from a king or president for he has no authority to change the message by adding to or taking from it; he must present it to the recipient pure without changes. As ambassadors for Christ, we must share the Pure Word of our King, or it will not be Christ the Living Word we are sharing but our powerless words instead.

Our witnessing, teaching, or preaching will be more effective if we try our best to be accurate and clear in explaining the Scriptures to help others understand what they need to do for salvation. This requires much prayer and study for there are many denominations which give various interpretations to the same Scriptures, and some even give opposite meanings for the same Scripture verse. The various Bible translations also disagree on many Scriptures, and satan is working with these differences as hard as he can to create as much confusion as possible. Even with all of these differences in interpretations, we are still the most blessed generation to have so many very smart people's interpretations of what the original texts or versions say in our different copies of the Bible that we can use along with concordances and other research materials as we pray and seek the Lord for the correct meanings of Scriptures. The scary part is that we are all going to be held personally accountable for whether we have made the effort to seek God's Pure Word regardless of what our denominations and preachers tell us. Ministers will hold up Bibles this coming Sunday and shout, **"I believe every word of the Bible,"** to stir up their congregations emotionally to help strengthen their congregation's confidence in the Bible, and to hopefully cause financial contributions to increase. If you ask them, **"Which specific copy or version are you referring to?"** they will eventually state they are referring to the original texts while knowing that those texts are hid away from us in sealed vaults of big churches in Europe. The real truth is that we do not have a perfect, Word of God, Bible available to us for study today. Does that relieve us of our responsibility to seek and learn to hear God's voice? No! Jesus states in *John 10:5, 14, and 27, "And a stranger will they not follow, but will flee from him: for they know not the voice of strangers. (14) I am the good shepherd, and know my sheep, and am known of mine. (27) My sheep hear my voice, and I know them, and they follow me."* The disciples and early Christians only had the Old Testament to study because most of the books of the New Testament had not been written or were in letter form to specific churches. Yet they were expected to learn, to hear, and to follow Jesus even as we are even though they were without our advantage of New Testament Scriptures. Regardless of the differences of interpretations by denominations and the different versions of our Bibles, we each still have the personal responsibility to seek and learn to hear God's "voice," and we will also be held accountable for our efforts or lack of efforts at the Judgment Seat of Christ.

Any minister as mentioned above that will state he believes every word of the Bible, regardless of the copy he is holding, either has not read the whole Bible, is lacking comprehension abilities, or does not have the courage to tell people what is in the Bible. Because, in one book alone where the Scripture states, *"Thus saith the Lord,"* God says that He does not know everything, and that is exactly opposite the world Christian view and probably ninety-nine percent of the non-Christians' view of God also. I have heard many

GOD'S LOVE   TO MANKIND

people say, *"I wouldn't have a God that didn't know everything. What kind of God would that be?"* If you say that, and you are one who also says that your God is the God of the Bible, then you better start seeking and searching the Bible to find out what kind of God the God of the Bible is because He is not being taught correctly from the Scriptures by our Christian community. Correcting that one error in belief about God will change the whole image of God that is presently being taught in our society, and when you find out why God does not know everything, you will see it is because of His great love for us. It is too long to explain in this writing so read my book, *"Prayer Changes Things,"* and you will be blessed and excited to know that God loves us so much He voluntarily gave up His right to know certain things about us. It is not my opinion; it is in black and white in the different versions of the Bible, and I did not put it in your Bible; it has been there all the time.

I have found in searching for specific definitions of many of the biblical words like faith, trust, mercy, grace, and charity that many of the biblical dictionaries use the intermingling of the other undefined words and a lot of good sounding expressions to define the first word, then use the first word to define the words that were used to define it. This circular method of defining or trying to define words actually leaves all of the words undefined without a specific meaning. I am looking at the definition of "grace" given in a very highly respected theological dictionary, and in different places it states, *"Divine favour or grace," "favour bestowed," "finding favour with God is finding grace," " to indue with Divine favour or grace,"* and in *Luke 1:28* the expression, *"highly favoured"* is stated as equivalent with being endued with grace. All of these expressions of grace or favour are stating that favour and grace are essentially interchangeable, and this will be shown to be totally incorrect in the following chapters on Mercy and Grace because favour is an expression of relationship with mercy -- *not grace*! The definition I am looking at also states that some of the Scriptures use the word grace as a testimony of the Deity of Christ. We Christians received grace at salvation, and it does not imply any deity to us, and besides there is no need for a testimony of the Deity of Christ: Christ is the Living Word of God, the third part of the Trinity, that lived in Jesus and in Christians' hearts and lives today, as the Apostle Paul states in *Colossians 1:27, "...Christ in you, the hope of glory."* Also, Christ as the Living Word of God, the Holy Spirit, is mentioned referring to Moses in *Hebrews 11:26, "Esteeming the reproach of Christ greater riches than the treasures in Egypt..."* Christ, the Living Word of God, created the heavens, earth and all of God's living creatures when God spoke in Genesis; there is no need to question the Deity of Christ if the word Christ is used correctly. Adding this incorrect discussion about the Deity of Christ in the definition of grace along with the other errors stated above equating grace and favor shows how terrible the theological understanding of Biblical grace is in the Christian community. The author was probably referring to the Deity of Jesus, instead of Christ. In this same Biblical Dictionary, the definition given for mercy uses incorrect references to grace, and there is no attempt to even try to define charity; it just says 'refer to love.' I will show you how to find the true meaning of these words and others in the following discussions.

The best way to understand the word meanings in the Scriptures is to pray and seek with an honest open heart and look for Scriptures which explain or define the correct Biblical use of the words. We cannot just sit down and decide we are going to logically figure out these words or concepts. God will have to open our eyes even to see the three Scriptures I mentioned above where

God says He does not know everything. **For example:** Just think of all the people who profess to read the complete Bible through each year, and all the ministers who have taught in seminaries, colleges, and churches for years, and all of the smart men and women who have worked on interpreting and translating all of the different copies of the Bible, adding all of these people would result in millions of Christians who should be aware of the above three verses I referred to where God says He does not know everything. But God did not open their eyes to see what the verses actually said or to the importance of what the verses said as they read the Scriptures if they were not with an open heart seeking for the truth when they read the verses. The translators had to have seen the verses, but I guess they just ignored them and did their specific jobs. If we are not seeking with a true heart, God will not open our eyes to His Word even though He wants us to know His Pure Word. When we do find how the Scriptures define or explain words, the centuries of intellectual changes which the devil has caused through society will be minimized, and we will get a much better understanding of the Scriptures. In my book, *"God Loved Esau,"* I show how one simple error in punctuation has caused people to believe for over twenty centuries that God said He hated Esau, when in reality God never said He hated Esau, and God loved Esau as much as He loves you, me, and everyone else. Millions of people through the years have read the verses about Esau, but God did not open their eyes to the truth because they either already had their minds made up that God said He hated Esau or they were not seeking truth with all their hearts. The devil is behind all of these errors and confusion for his whole purpose is to block God's true loving image to mankind, and at the same time to confuse mankind from seeing the true loving relationship God wants us to have with Him as Jesus says in J*ohn 10:10, "The thief cometh not, but for to steal, and to kill, and to destroy: I am come that they might* *have life, and that they might have it more abundantly."* I truly believe that if the Pure Word of God and God's true loving image were being taught correctly in our society that we would not have to worry or concern ourselves with the crooked politicians in Washington, D.C. for they would want to be Christians too. All of mankind is looking to fill the empty agonizing void in their hearts which only the Spirit of Christ, the Living Word Christ can fill. But non-Christians in our society can barely see a glimpse of His Loving Glory in our mixed-up confused Christian community because of all the false teachings supported by the many groups and denominations who in pride say, **" I was born a ****, raised a **** and will die a ****, nothing is going to change me."** I am glad the Apostle Paul was more open minded than that and changed his beliefs on the road to Damascus when Jesus told him of the error in his beliefs.

The Apostle Paul states in Ephesians that all of our ministers of all denominations are supposed to be seeking to bring Christianity together into the unity of ONE faith. He states in *Ephesians 4:4-5, 13, "There is one body, and one Spirit, even as ye are called in one hope of your calling; (5) One Lord, ONE FAITH, one baptism. (13) Till we all come in the unity of the faith, and of the knowledge of the Son of God, unto a perfect man, unto the measure of the stature of the fullness of Christ."* Ministers trying to bring us all together in one true faith is not happening in our country, but it must if we are to survive as a nation based on Godly principles. God has put up with Christian laziness and pride long enough, and it is evident He is not standing up for us now by the fact that He is not protecting us against the onslaughts of the devil who uses ungodly organizations such as the ACLU, most of the members of our congress, federal judges and President. If Christians were truly seeking the truth and love of God to share with others, God would be working such great signs and wonders in our society that most of the above people would also want to turn to Him too. We Christians have indirectly caused the problems in our society because the ungodly acts of our society only reflect our failure to share correctly as God's ambassadors His great love for mankind in truth. The nation Israel was supposed to have been God's priests or representatives to all the earth from the time they became a nation, and they failed their calling also. Unless the Christian community will come together and seek the true one faith, we will no longer exist as the *Christian Nation the U.S. Supreme Court declared us to be in 143 U.S 457; 12 S. Ct 511; 36 L. Ed 226; Feb 29, 1892, "...These and many other matters which might be noticed, add a volume of unofficial declarations to the mass of organic utterances that this is a Christian nation."* Since this declaration by our U.S. Supreme Court has never been overturned, we still are legally a Christian Nation, but only in the sense that our founding, governing documents are based on Christian principles of respect, freedom, individual opportunity, and compassion for others around the world. Our country has never been run by Christians as a "Christian" nation like Muslims and other religious groups have set up and controlled their countries. Throughout history no other nation has ever offered the personal freedoms and opportunities for seeking fulfillment in life to its citizens that have been available in our country. But lately it seems like so many who have left the bad situations in their place of birth have come to our country and are trying to change it to the political and religious restrictions of where they came from instead of meshing into our society and enjoying with us their new life of freedoms here. We cannot retain our Christian Nation status of individual respect and freedoms by only fighting social problems and expecting the government to correct the problems; we Christians must seek God's Pure Word in unity so the Lord can clean up the Christian community first, then He will back us up as we go forth in unity teaching and preaching His Pure Living Word, Christ. Only changed hearts submitted to God will be able to change our nation to love and respect for each other regardless of race or religion because there is too much money being made by the leaders of both the religious and political groups by the divisiveness presently in our society.

I am going to show or explain to you how to read and study the Bible to obtain more meaning from the Scriptures if you are truly seeking God with all your heart. I am going to discuss Mercy, Grace, and Charity because as I have mentioned in various writings we cannot understand other aspects of God's Word if we do not understand the fundamentals. After the discussion of charity, I will include a couple of miscellaneous subjects which can be understood more clearly after understanding charity. The first subject I will discuss after charity is the gifts of the Spirit, and then of all things, SIN! You may wonder 'Why sin,' but you will see that the devil hates the word *charity* so much that he has had it left out of all of the new Bible versions for phony reasons. Charity is supposedly archaic, too old, not used in our society, old-fashioned, etc. Yet, we have thousands of active charitable organizations and charitable events that are taking place daily in our society, so is charity unused or old-fashioned? No! Those are not the reasons charity has been left out of the new versions. The devil has caused the word, charity, which expresses the most beautiful work of God's love in union with His children to be removed from all of the modern Bible versions. Not only because charity shows the beauty of God's outreach to mankind through His children, but the understanding of the word charity also allows for a much clearer understanding of sin which the devil does not want mankind to know. So by removing charity from the most popular modern versions of the Bible, the devil has achieved two goals: to block some of the true loving image of God to mankind and to cover up from mankind the seriousness of what is actually sin.

MERCY

Mercy is simply a one way love that does not require any specific response either positive or negative, but naturally, if a response is necessary, the positive response is desired. One of the best examples of mercy is shown in the story Jesus told of the good Samaritan in *Luke 10:30–37*. The story tells of a man who was traveling from Jerusalem to Jericho. The man was beaten, robbed, and left half-dead beside the road. A priest and a Levite, considered to be godly leaders, passed by and did not take the time to help the wounded man beside the road. A Samaritan came by and had compassion on the hurt man. The Samaritan bound hurt man's wounds, took him to an inn, paid for his stay at the inn, left additional money to pay for him to stay longer to get well if needed, and promised to pay more if it cost more than the money he left. Jesus then asked the lawyer, *"Which now of these three, thinkest thou, was neighbour unto him that fell among the thieves?"* The lawyer answered, *"He that shewed mercy on him."* The lawyer evidently used the word mercy in the proper manner for that day. Therefore, we need to look at why the word mercy was chosen instead of some other word.

First, we see that the Samaritan did not make any kind of deal with the hurt man, asking him to pay him back for his help. Also, it appears the hurt man was probably a Jew, since the story indicates the priest and Levite should have stopped to help. If the hurt man were a Jew, many people of the two races hated each other so much, as with racial problems in our society today, that the man might not have even let the Samaritan help him if he had been conscious. But the Samaritan loved "others" so much that he stopped to help the hurt man,

MERCY GRACE CHARITY
GOD'S LOVE ⚜ TO MANKIND

probably of another race, without asking, expecting, or requiring any response from the hurt man to pay him back or show his appreciation in any way for his efforts. These Scriptures show mercy to be the one-way love to others which does not require any form of response.

The Apostle Paul states that God blesses lost people, non-Christians, and even disobedient Christians to draw them to repentance in *Romans 2:4, "Or despises thou the riches of His goodness and forbearance and longsuffering; not knowing that the goodness of God leadeth thee to repentance?"* This action, the Love of God toward disobedient mankind, is called "unmerited favor," mercy. God is always reaching out in His mercy trying to draw us to Him, or back to Him, as long as we are alive, and He does not demand or require a positive response, although He desires it. God states in *Ezekiel 33:11, "Say unto them, As I live, saith the Lord God, I have no pleasure in the death of the wicked; but that the wicked turn from his way and live: turn ye, turn ye from your evil ways; for why will ye die, O house of Israel?"* Probably most of the time people in pride claim that it is through their own hard work and abilities that the blessings happened, and God does not get credit or thanks from them for His blessings to them.

God blesses people through His mercy to try to get them to turn to Him because of His Love, for He could make us all turn to Him if He wanted to, but while we are here on earth He wants us to voluntarily choose Him. Although, there is coming a time after our death on earth when God says He will force everyone who has not bowed their knees to Him here to bow their knees in judgment as in *Isaiah 45:23; Romans 14:11, and in Philippians 2:10, "That at the name of Jesus every knee should bow, of things in heaven, and things in earth, and things under the earth; (11) And that every tongue should confess that Jesus Christ is Lord, to the glory of God the Father."*

Jesus spoke many times of us sharing His Word and love in a positive manner with those around us who may treat us badly or who will not respond positively to our outreach. We must expect that in many cases the responses from others to God's direct mercy to them or God's mercy through us to them will be negative for Jesus said in *John 15:18, "If the world hate you, ye know that it hated me before it hated you,"* and in *Matthew 5:11-12, "Blessed are ye, when men shall revile you, and persecute you, and shall say all manner of evil against you falsely, for my sake. (12) Rejoice, and be exceeding glad: for great is your reward in heaven: for so persecuted they the prophets which were before you."* Read carefully the following verses from the book of Luke, Chapter 6. In the last verse below, Jesus asks us to be merciful as our Father is merciful. Therefore, Jesus is stating that this outward, one-way outreach, expecting or requiring nothing in return, is what He expects from us, too. We must submit ourselves and allow Him to work through us as He desires and states in,

Luke 6:27-36,

(27) "But I say unto you which hear, Love your enemies, do good to them which hate you,

(28) Bless them that curse you, and pray for them which despitefully use you.

(29) And unto him that smiteth thee on the one cheek offer also the other; and him that taketh away thy cloke forbid not to take thy coat also.

(30)   Give to every man that asketh of thee; and of him
         hat taketh away thy goods ask them not again.
(31)   And as ye would that men should do to you,
         do ye also to them likewise.

(32)   For if ye love them which love you, what thank
         have ye? For sinners also love those that love them.

(33)   And if ye do good to them which do good to you,
         what thank have ye? For sinners also do even
         the same.

(34)   And if ye lend to them of whom ye hope to
         receive, what thank have ye? For sinners also
         lend to sinners, to receive as much again.

(35)   But love ye your enemies, and do good, and lend,
         hoping for nothing again; and your reward
         shall be great, and ye shall be the children of the
         Highest: for He is kind unto the unthankful and
         to the evil.

(36)   Be ye therefore merciful, as your Father also
         is merciful."

These Scriptures also show that mercy is the one-way love, or God, working through His people toward an ungrateful, unthankful, and evil people. God wants us to allow Him through His Spirit to work through us to the lost world, but if we allow personal grudges, unforgiveness, or other bad thoughts and feelings about those people to control us, then God will not be able to use us for them as He desires. Jesus, in verse 36, instructs us to be merciful as our Father is merciful which means to allow Him to keep reaching out through us to the ungodly people around us regardless of their response. The Scriptures remind us that we were all ungodly people in our past. The Apostle Paul states in *Ephesians 2:2–5, "Wherein in time past ye walked according to the course of this world, according to the prince of the power of the air, the spirit that now worketh in the children of disobedience: (3) Among whom also we all had our conversation in times past in the lusts of our flesh, fulfilling the desires of the flesh and of the mind; and were by nature the children of wrath, even as others. (4) But God, who is rich in mercy, for His great love wherewith He loved us, (5) Even when we were dead in sins, hath quickened us together with Christ, (by grace ye are saved)."*

For God to use us to share Himself or mercy through us to others, we must keep our hearts clean of unforgiveness, prejudices, and envy like the garden hose must be free of kinks, dirt, and other obstructions for water to flow freely. We must have a cleansed heart free of the kinks of rebellion, laziness, prejudices or other sins for God's Spirit to flow freely through us. Jesus states in *Matthew 5:7, "Blessed are the merciful: for they shall obtain mercy."* When we allow God to work through us and show mercy, He will then give us mercy in our time of need, but if we intentionally through our judgmental attitude refuse to show mercy to others, then God may withhold mercy in our time of need. We all need God's mercy every day so we should try to learn to show others mercy even though it is not very easy most of the time. It would be a lot easier if we could slap some of them on the head a couple of times first, then show the mercy; but what if God did the same to us and slapped us on the head first before showing us mercy? There are so many things that God does for us daily through His mercy for which we do not know or thank Him. He protects us at night on the highways, from bad foods, from bad air, from so many potentially harmful situations. He is working for us even though we are not even aware of His help, and in *Psalms 136 the Scriptures states twenty-six times in twenty-six verses, "His mercy endureth forever."* Therefore, we must conclude *"His mercy endureth forever."* It is only through God's great mercies that we are *not destroyed by satan, for Jesus says in John 10:10, "The thief cometh not, but for to steal, and to kill, and to destroy: I am come that they might have life, and that they might have it more abundantly,"* and *Lamentations 3:22-23 states, "It is of the Lord's mercies that we are not consumed, because His compassions fail not. (23) They are new every morning: great is Thy faithfulness."*

God has forgiven us and has shown so much mercy in our lives, and now He wants us to love Him enough that we will allow Him to work through us to reach others who have turned from Him as spoken of in *Romans 1:21, 24, 26, 28, "Because that, when they knew God, they glorified Him not as God, neither were thankful; but became vain in their imaginations, and their foolish heart was darkened. (24) Wherefore God also gave them up to uncleanness through the lusts of their own hearts, ... (26) For this cause God gave them up unto vile affections: ... (28) And even as they did not like to retain God in their knowledge, God gave them over to a reprobate mind (not knowing right from wrong), to do those things which are not convenient."* God has not given them up for salvation, and He never will, but He wants to use us and the testimony of His great works in our lives to cause them to want to come to Him. He is trying to indirectly approach them through us in ways which will not cause them in their pride to push Him further out of their lives as they did when He first revealed Himself to them and approached them directly. To do this, God wants to use His blessings to us as a testimony for them so they will see what they are missing in hope that they will turn to Him. During the Old Testament period, the country Israel was supposed to have been God's testimony on earth to draw all other peoples of the earth to Him as stated in *Psalms 67:1-2, "God be merciful unto us, and bless us; and cause His face to shine upon us; Selah. (2) That Thy way may be known upon earth, Thy saving health among all nations."* Israel failed to properly represent God, and our Christian society is also failing because our testimony of God and His character is so mixed with error, untruth, and fables that His glory is not shining through to draw the lost people to desire Christ because of all the confusion. Goodness and mercy spoken of in *Psalms 23:6, "Surely goodness and mercy shall follow me all the days of my life:..."* are not our two angels following us to care for us as most preachers indicate, for goodness and mercy to follow us, we must be allowing God to work His Spirit through us to show His goodness and mercy to others. Do we love God and appreciate Him enough for all He has done for us that we will still minister to those who despitefully use us and curse us, or do we misuse the Scriptures in *Mark 6:11 and Luke 9:5* that speaks of 'brushing the dust from our feet' to readily turn from people who reject us from any of our future concern or witness? Never give up witnessing to anyone because an honest, positive witness is a means of God working through His grace in us to show mercy to them. The Scriptures state in *Psalms 18:25 and Matthew 5:7 that those who show mercy will receive mercy* and in *James 2:13 the Scripture states, "For he shall have judgment without mercy, that hath shewed no mercy;..."* We must make the choice to show mercy, and if we show mercy from a pure heart of love for others, then we can be assured that God is keeping record of it in a Book of Remembrance, and He doesn't juggle the books. When we die, we cannot take anything with us, but there are things we can send ahead that might be used as "building blocks" for our "mansions," such as, our mercy, giving to the poor, our prayers, our praise, and several other things. If God doesn't show us mercy in heaven, and He only uses the materials we send ahead some of us at best might only have "shacks." God delights in mercy, *Micah 7:18-19,"Who is a God like unto Thee, that pardoneth iniquity, and passeth by the transgression of the remnant of His heritage? He retaineth not His anger for ever, because He delighteth in mercy. (19) He will turn again, He will have compassion upon us; He will subdue our iniquities; and thou wilt cast all their sins into the depths of the sea."* If we knew our earthly father delighted in some activity like fishing, golf, or hunting, we would probably do everything we could to try to imitate him so we could be closer to him and receive his praise. Our heavenly Father will certainly delight in us when we, because of our love for Him, choose to submit ourselves to the ridicule of others to let His Spirit work through us to reach out to them. Make a commitment today to start showing mercy, cheerfully, to others even though like us they definitely do not deserve it, for if they deserved it, it *would not be mercy, Romans 12:8, "Or he that exhorteth, on exhortation: he that giveth, let him do it with simplicity; he that ruleth, with diligence; he that sheweth mercy, with cheerfulness."*

People of the Old Testament only had God's mercy and truth, (God's Word), because they did not have the relationship of God in them which is called grace like we do. *Psalms 25:10 states, "All the paths of the Lord are mercy and truth unto such as keep His covenant and His testimonies."* There was a lot of punishment and curses for those who disobeyed God, but only mercy and truth for His people seeking to obey and follow Him. Jesus compared our new relationship of the Spirit in us to the Old Testament relationship of God with or to them in *Mark 7:28* when speaking of John the

Baptist, *"For I say unto you, Among those that are born of women there is not a greater prophet than John the Baptist: but he that is least in the kingdom of God is greater than he."*

When we see the word mercy in the Scriptures, we should always think of the outward work of the Spirit of God to mankind such as in our lives when we see God's providential intervention to save people's lives in accidents, to cause good things to happen in time of need when we or our loved ones have not specifically prayed for the happening, or good circumstances which prevent bad things from happening, etc. Many times God in His mercy allows our cars to breakdown at a convenient location for us to be safe or for the cars to be fixed, and sometimes He keeps them running miraculously when they should not even continue to run by natural means. God in His mercy works things out for special meetings with people whom we need for our edification, or in our businesses, or for us to witnesses to or help in their time of need. These are examples of God's mercy that works through His Spirit externally to mankind, but not in our hearts. Our relationship to God with Christ in our hearts is greater than the relationship God had with any of the people of the Old Testament as Jesus pointed out when talking about John the Baptist. Notice in Ephesians 2:1-5, quoted earlier, that when the Apostle Paul was talking about out past sins and how awful we were, he used the word mercy for God's love. But, when he mentioned Christ and salvation, the corresponding word he chose to use to describe God's love was grace which leads to our next often misused word that needs to be discussed: grace.

GRACE

G od states in *Isaiah 45:5, 6, 18, 21, 23* "*...I am the Lord, and there is none else... (21)* "*...and there is no God else beside me; a just God and a Saviour; there is none beside me,*" and in *(23) I have sworn by myself, the Word is gone out of my mouth in righteousness, and shall not return, 'That unto me every knee shall bow, every tongue shall swear.*" The Apostle Paul states in *Philippians 2:9-11 that the man Jesus has been exalted to equality with God, "Wherefore God also hath highly exalted Him, and given Him a name which is above every name: (10) That at the name of Jesus every knee should bow, of things in heaven, and things in earth, and things under the earth; (11) And that every tongue should confess that Jesus Christ is Lord, to the glory of God the Father,*" and Paul states in *1 Timothy 2:4-5,* that God our Saviour, *"Who will have all men to be saved, and to come unto the knowledge of the truth. (5) For there is one God, and one mediator between God and men, the man Christ Jesus."* The Apostle Paul recognizes that Jesus, the man who died *on the cross, has been exalted to equality with God when He states in Colossians 3:20, "Now a mediator is not a mediator of one, but God is one."* Christ, the Living Word of God in Jesus, did not die on the cross; the man Jesus died on the cross. Paul had already explained the relationship between Jesus and the Father in....

> *Colossians 1:12-19,*
> *(12)   "Giving thanks unto the Father, which hath made us meet to be partakers of the inheritance of the saints in light:*

(13)   *Who hath delivered us from the power of darkness, and hath translated us into the kingdom of His dear Son:*

14)   *In whom we have redemption through His blood, even the forgiveness of sins:*

(15)   *Who (Jesus) is the image of the invisible God, the firstborn of every creature:*

(16)   *For by Him were all things created, that are in heaven, and that are in earth, visible and invisible, whether they be thrones, or dominions, or principalities, or powers: all things were created by Him, and for Him:*

(17)   *And He is before all things, and by Him all things consist.*

(18)   *And He is the head of the body, the church, who is the beginning, the firstborn from the dead; that in all things He might have the preeminence.*

(19)   *For it pleased the Father that in Him should all fullness dwell,"*

And in *Colossians 2:9* *"For in Him (Jesus) dwelleth all the fullness of the Godhead bodily."* The man Jesus has been exalted by the Father to equality with the Father as the third manifestation of God in the Trinity: Father, Son Jesus, and Christ who is the Living Word that we often call the Holy Spirit.

Grace is any work of God, God's love, the Holy Spirit, or the Spirit of Christ in our hearts. There is only one God and one Spirit; therefore, by whatever name we use to call God, any work of God in the heart of mankind is grace or what we call a work of grace. We call God the Comforter when He brings comfort in our hearts; we call Him the Spirit of faith when we have received the Spirit of His manifested Word to us in our hearts. After we have received to faith the Spirit of His manifested Words into our hearts, we call Him or His Living Word in our hearts the Spirit of Grace; we call Him the Spirit of Truth or Teacher when He reveals knowledge, understanding, or wisdom to us about Himself or the Scriptures. We refer to God as the Holy Spirit or Holy Ghost when we recognize His movement through events to get our attention or to guide us; but, however, we identify God working, if it is any kind of work of God in our hearts, we call the movement grace, or a work of grace. The total simple definition of grace is "The work of God in the hearts of mankind." The following Scriptures will show the beauty, complexity, greatness, *gfeeojgjrheeooldkdjkr,* and the all encompassing perfection of the creative work of God manifesting Himself as the Spirit of Love in our hearts which we call grace. We will first look at the changed heart which God creates in us at salvation to make us a new creation. *Gfeeojgjrheeoolkddjkr* is defined as all of those other great attributes or characteristics of God working in our hearts which are either unknown to me or are too great for me to understand or describe about grace. This is called speaking in unknown type.

In Mathematics or Science when we find two objects which are equal to a third object, we know then that the first two objects must be equal to each other. For example: If 2 + 2 equals 4, and 1 + 3 equals 4, then we know that 2 plus 2 MUST equal 1 plus 3, and they do; therefore, they are equal. Now to

GOD'S LOVE   TO MANKIND

use that simple logic to study grace, we know there is only one way to be saved as stated in *Ephesians 2:8, "For by grace are ye saved through faith..."* Therefore, every other Scripture which states a means or description of salvation will not be saying there is a different way to be saved, but they will be discussing a new aspect of grace from a different viewpoint, for we know there is only one way to be saved and that is by grace. Also, since the above Scripture states that grace saves us, and grace follows the result of our accepting God's Word to faith, then all of the other Scriptures discussing salvation must be following or be the result of the action or work of our faith as the Apostle Paul states in *Romans 5:2, "By whom also we have access by faith into this grace wherein we stand, and rejoice in hope of the glory of God."* From this verse we see that grace is not just poured into some people's hearts and others left to struggle and wonder if God will ever send or give them grace, for that would be more like mercy when God intervenes periodically in different ways to different people as the Apostle Paul states in *Romans 9:15, "For He saith to Moses, I will have mercy on whom I will have mercy, and I will have compassion on whom I will have compassion."* Grace always follows our faith which comes from our free-will choice to accept into our hearts and obey God's Word to faith that He has revealed to us. Grace follows faith because when God reveals something to us through His Spirit, the Living Word, and we accept His Living Word; the Living Word comes into our hearts and becomes the Spirit of Grace to perform the action in us that God spoke to us, and we accepted into our hearts to faith. We grow in faith and grace every time we accept and receive God's Word in our hearts by faith and it then performs a work of grace in us. We can make a free will choice to accept God's Words of instruction, correction, comfort, forgiveness, or salvation to faith and receive God's Living Words into our hearts to perform a work of grace any time we choose. Even now as you are reading this material, hopefully, you are receiving God's Words into your heart, and you are growing in faith and grace. Grace is available, plenteous, and sufficient to cleanse any repentant heart that will cry out to God for forgiveness and invite His Spirit to come in, *Romans 5:20, "Moreover the law entered, that the offence might abound. But where sin abounded, grace did much more abound."* God is greater than all our sins! God does not stop working through His Spirit in our hearts after we receive His Spirit into our hearts for salvation. He continues to move in our hearts, but only as we receive more of His Living Word through faith to grace in our hearts as we grow or mature in our walk with the Lord as a Christian. That is why we need to be reading and studying His Word, attending worship services and Bible studies, and doing everything we can to be available and allow Him every opportunity to fill us with His Word so we can become more like Jesus. Also, another important comment about the above verse, in Ephesians 2:8, is that **"saved"** is referring to the process of us being forgiven of our sins, becoming children of God, and all the rest of the events and actions which must take place in our hearts by the work of His Spirit of Grace to make us eligible and guarantee that we go to heaven, instead of us having to pay the price of our sins for an eternity in the Lake of Fire. Therefore, in the Scriptures we discuss or analyze, being **"saved"** is the same as *"being Born Again," "becoming children or sons of God," "becoming a new creatures in Christ Jesus," "being converted," "becoming one of His,"* or any other references to when we receive the new changed hearts as we enter the body of Christ.

The Apostle Paul states in *2 Timothy 3:16, "All Scripture is given by inspiration of God, and is profitable for doctrine, for reproof, for correction, for instruction in righteousness."* When I state that a Scripture is one of my favorites, I am only saying that God has maybe given me more understanding of a particular Scripture, and I like to share it or am able to share it easier when witnessing to others; I do not think any one Scripture is greater than another because all are God's Words. Therefore, one of my favorite Scriptures that I like to use to explain the "saving" grace of *Ephesians 2:8* is God's Words spoken through the prophet in *Ezekiel 36:26-27, "A new heart also will I give you, and a new Spirit will I put within you: and I will take away the stony heart out of your flesh, and I will give you an heart of flesh. (27) And I will put my Spirit within you, and cause you to walk in my statutes, and ye shall keep my judgments, and do them."* God is promising us a new heart and that He will actually put His Spirit that will be new to us, in us. This is not the result of someone making a decision that they are going to start living good by going to church, or by someone just going forward in church, answering a couple questions, and getting baptized in water. God only replies to a full whole-hearted cry of the heart for forgiveness as stated in *Deuteronomy 4:29 and Jeremiah 29:13 which states, "And ye shall seek me, and find me; when ye shall search for me with all your heart."* Also the Scriptures state in *Job 33:27-28, "He (God) looketh upon men, and if any say, I have sinned, and perverted that which was right, and it profited me not; (28) He (God) will deliver his soul from going into the pit, and his life shall see the light."* We must all call out to God through Jesus like the Old Testament people called direct to God for salvation, but when we call, we not only receive forgiveness of our sins but we also receive the cleansing from our sins. We receive a new heart; we receive the Spirit of Christ in our hearts, and we are adopted or engrafted into the family of God as His children. The grace for salvation includes all of the actions, efforts, and creative work God performs by His Spirit of Christ in us to create all of these great changes in us. God says He will create a new heart in us and throw out the old one. It doesn't matter how hardened a person's heart is before salvation; God says He is going to change us and start us all off in our new life as one of His children with a new clean heart. The Apostle Paul had a fantastic change in his heart immediately when he met Jesus, and he states in *2 Corinthians 5:17, "Therefore if any man be in Christ, he is a new creature: old things are passed away; behold, all things are become new."* We do not grow into becoming a Christian; we become a Christian the instant God puts the Spirit of His Son into our hearts to engraft us into His family. When His Spirit, Christ, enters our hearts, we are changed from being just a creation of God to being children of God; we are born again by the Spirit of God into the family of God; we are saved; we become a new creature with a new Spirit and a new, clean heart! I had so much hate and fear in my heart when I received the Spirit of Christ and my new heart that I knew immediately something remarkable had happened in me that I could not have done of myself. With the new heart, God also promises to put in us a "new" Spirit. This new Spirit He puts in us is the promise of the Father that Jesus told the disciples to wait for on the Day of Pentecost in *Acts 1:4-5, "...but wait for the promise of the Father, which, saith He, ye have heard of me. (5) For John truly baptized with water; but ye shall be baptized with the Holy Ghost not many days hence."* The Apostle Paul states in *Romans 8:9, "But ye are not in the flesh, but in the Spirit, if so be that the Spirit of God dwell in you. Now if any man have not the Spirit of Christ, he is none of His."* Without the Spirit of Christ in us, we are still one of His created creatures, but we are none of His family, and we are not a Christian. We might be very good people like Cornelius and his family in *Acts Chapter 10,* but also like Cornelius, we are not a Christian regardless of how good we are if we do not have the Spirit of Christ in our hearts. So do not think every good person you meet, even if they attend a "church," must be a Christian, and then let that cause you to hold back or fail to witness to them about salvation just because they seem so good and go to church. If you want to be right more than you are wrong, consider those you meet, for witnessing purposes, a non-Christian until you hear their personal testimony of their changed heart. Always seek to hear people's personal testimony of their changed heart before you stop being overly concerned about their salvation and sharing the salvation gospel to them, especially if they happen to be ministers. The changed heart which Christ creates in us and the new Spirit God puts in us are the greatest evidences of our being a Christian, for almost all good works can also be done by good Cornelius type non-Christians which Jesus tells us about in *Matthew 7:22-23, "Many will say to me in that day, Lord, Lord, have we not prophesied in thy mane? And in thy name have cast our devils? And in thy name done many wonderful works? (13) And then will I profess unto them, I never knew you: depart from me, ye that work iniquity."* The dividing line between being a Christian and a non-Christian is the instant when we receive the Spirit of Christ into our hearts. The Spirit that God puts in us will be new to us but not new to God because it will be God Himself coming to live in us by putting His Spirit, Christ the Living Word, in us. A few times in the Gospels Jesus even referred to the Spirit in Him as being the Father in Him as in *John 14:10-11, "Believest thou not that I am in the Father, and the Father in me? The Words that I speak unto you I speak not of myself: but the Father that dwelleth in me, He doeth the works. (11) Believe me that I am in the Father, and the Father in me:..."* Christians who have received Christ the Living Word into their hearts should or will have an evidence of hunger in their heart for reading and studying God's Word for God loves His Word so much He has exalted it above all His names in *Psalms 138:2*. "Christ in us" will put His love in us for His Word. "Christ in us" is also the essence of the New Covenant between God and man which was a mystery to the Old Testament people who could not understand 'God in us' as the Apostle Paul states in *Colossians 1:27, "To whom God would make known what is the riches of the glory of this mystery among the Gentiles; which is Christ in you, the hope of glory."*

In the beginning when God spoke, His Living Word, Christ, created light, mankind, and all the other creatures and creation of God. The Apostle Paul stated in *1 Corinthians 1:24, "...Christ the power of God, and the wisdom of God."* Christ the Living Word of God is the all-powerful creator of the Universe, and Christ being the Living Word of God is pure wisdom of God. *Proverbs 3:19 states, "The Lord by wisdom hath founded the earth...,"* therefore, Christ the Living Word of God is the Wisdom of God, and they are identical since both created God's creation. Also, Christ, the all-powerful creator arm of God, is the power that Jesus told the disciples to wait for on the day of Pentecost when He told them to wait for the promise of the Father; Jesus said to them in *Acts 1:4-5,8, "...wait for the promise of the Father, which, saith He, ye have heard of me. (5) For John truly baptized with water; but ye shall be baptized with the Holy Ghost not many days hence. (8) But ye shall receive power, after that the Holy Ghost is come upon you:..."* In the Greek, the word power of *1 Corinthians 1:24* above is the same as the word power in *Acts 1:8*, so Jesus was telling the disciples to wait for the '**promise of the Father**' discussed above in *Ezekiel 36:26* where God promised He would put a new Spirit and a new hearts in us. The disciples received the new Spirit, Christ, Who removed the stony hearts and gave them new cleansed baptized hearts which the Apostle Paul called the baptism of the Spirit into the body (of Christ) in *1 Corinthians 12:13, "For by one Spirit are we all baptized into one body, whether we be Jews or Gentiles, whether we be bond or free; and have been* *all made to drink into one Spirit."* The baptism of the Holy Ghost or Spirit is the baptism of the heart into the body of Christ at salvation which is also spoken of by the Apostle Peter in *1 Peter 3:21, "The like figure whereunto even baptism doth also now save us* **(not the putting away of the filth of the flesh, but the answer of a good conscience toward God,)** *by the resurrection of Jesus Christ."* The disciples received power, the Spirit of the Living Word, Christ, into their hearts, and they were baptized by the Spirit of Christ into the body of Christ as children of God on the Day of Pentecost. The disciples did not receive the Spirit of Christ into their hearts when Jesus spoke to them in J*ohn 20:22, (Greek) "And this saying He breathed in and says to them Receive ye Spirit Holy"* or *(KJV), "And when He had said this, He breathed on them, and saith unto them, Receive ye the Holy Ghost."* The Word of Faith and some Pentecostal groups teach that when Jesus breathed on the disciples in the KJV that Jesus actually breathed the Holy Spirit or the Spirit of Christ into the disciples' hearts for their salvation at that time and that they were "saved" at that time. By teaching that the disciples received God's Spirit into their hearts and were saved in *John 20:22*, then it is possible for them to teach that the Day of Pentecost experience would be a "second blessing" from God called the "Baptism of the Holy Spirit." That is twisting Scriptures to meet denominational beliefs because the Greek version stated above says only that Jesus breathed in and then spoke to the disciples. Also, none but Jesus had received the Spirit of Christ into their hearts before the Day of Pentecost when the New Covenant between God and mankind was initiated; the disciples did not have a different plan of salvation than we have.

Christ is the Spirit of God that lived in the man Jesus as shown in *John 1:1-2, 14, "In the beginning was the Word, and the Word was with God,*

*and the Word was God. (2) The same was in the beginning with God. (14)
And the Word was made flesh, and dwelt among us, (and we beheld His
glory, the glory as of the only begotten of the Father,) full of grace (the Living
Word, Christ, living and working in Jesus' heart) and truth (God's Word)."*
God, Christ the Living Word, is our savior who comes to us when we call out for
forgiveness and salvation to God through the name of Jesus, and we receive
the same Spirit of Christ in our hearts that lived in Jesus. At some time during
the process of God changing our hearts and putting His Spirit in us, the Apostle
Paul says we are adopted, or as the Apostle James states, we are "engrafted,"
into the family of God as stated by Paul in *Galatians 4:6-7, "And because ye
are sons, God hath sent forth the Spirit of His Son, (Christ), into your hearts,
crying, Abba, Father. (7) Wherefore thou art no more a servant, but a son;
and if a son, then an heir of God through Christ,"* and in *Romans 8:15-17*
Paul states, *"For ye have not received the spirit of bondage again to fear;
but ye have received the Spirit of adoption, whereby we cry, Abba, Father.
(16) The Spirit itself beareth witness with our spirit, that we are the children
of God: (17) And if children, then heirs; heirs of God, and joint-heirs with
Christ; if so be that we suffer with Him, that we may be also glorified
together."* Jesus' earthly brother, the Apostle James, states in *James 1:21,
"Wherefore lay apart all filthiness and superfluity of naughtiness, and receive
with meekness the engrafted Word, which is able to save your souls."* All
of these changes that God makes in us as He creates our new heart, puts His
Spirit into our hearts, makes us new creatures, adopts us, and engrafts us into
His family as His children are included as part of the work of grace or the
definition of grace. Grace just keeps getting bigger, better, and greater, and that
is only the part that we understand about what He does! How God actually
creates all of those fantastic changes in us is incomprehensible and similar to

a caterpillar one day just deciding that he is going to change to a beautiful butterfly, or a tad pole getting up one morning and deciding that today he will just make himself a frog. Neither we nor the caterpillar or tad pole could make those changes or even understand them, only God can!

When we call to God through Jesus for salvation, God allows Jesus to reply. Jesus speaks the Living Word, Christ, who was Jesus' Spirit into our hearts. Jesus is now God's speaker from heaven, as He was during His time here on earth, and Jesus' spoken Word that goes forth is the same all-powerful, creative Living Word, Christ, that God spoke in the beginning of creation as stated in *Hebrews 1:1-2, "God, who at sundry times and in divers manners spake in time past unto the fathers by the prophets, (2) Hath in these last days spoken unto us by His Son, whom He hath appointed heir of all things by whom also He made the worlds."* Jesus replies to our cry for forgiveness and salvation by speaking the "engrafted Word," the Living Word of God, Christ, to us. Grace includes all of the engrafting process which joins our new hearts to God through the Spirit of Christ and makes us His children at salvation. The Apostle Peter states we are "born again," or saved by the incorruptible Word of God in *1 Peter 1:23, "Being born again, not of corruptible seed, but of incorruptible, by the Word of God, which liveth and abideth for ever."* We must be preaching and teaching the incorruptible Word of God without error, for God in *Psalms 138:2* states that He has exalted His Word above all His names, and the Scriptures state in *Proverbs 30:5-6, "Every Word of God is pure: He is a shield unto them that put their trust in Him. (6) Add thou not unto His Words, lest He reprove thee, and thou be found a liar."* We have got to be careful to seek, find, and teach God's pure, incorruptible or engrafting Word, or God will not back up what we say and our listeners will be left without a true witness of God. Only the pure, incorruptible Word is Christ; and if we change the Word in any way, we corrupt the Word, and the word then is only our powerless word, not the all-powerful creating Word, Christ. Since we are saved by the incorruptible or engrafting Word in our hearts, that means we must have first heard those Living Words from God and accepted and received them to faith in our hearts. Those same Living Words we chose to accept to faith into our hearts now produce the work of grace in our hearts for salvation. Grace always is the result of us accepting God's Living Word that we hear into our hearts by faith. God does not put His Word into our hearts without us first making the choice in agreement with God to accept or receive His Words, and then by us actually inviting God's Spirit in for whatever He desires. Grace always follows our acceptance and obedience of God's Word to faith. If we hear God's Words of the gospel and then reject His Words or we decide to put off accepting, we will be in unbelief as discussed in *Hebrews 4:2, "For unto us was the gospel preached, as well as unto them: but the Word preached did not profit them, not being mixed with faith in them that heard it,"* and in *2 Thessalonians 2:10, "And with all deceivableness of unrighteousness in them that perish; because they received not the love of the truth, that they might be saved."* We do not "work" for our salvation, but we must humble ourselves to God's Word, repent of our sins, and call out to God through Jesus to forgive us and send His Spirit into our hearts to save us. He will not come into our hearts uninvited or if we try to hold part of our hearts back from Him so that we are asking Him to be our savior but not our Lord! That is a deception the devil has used to trick a lot of people into believing they can say words to be saved from hell by Jesus as their savior, but at the same time they do not have to surrender their hearts to Jesus as Lord of their lives.

One characteristic of the work of grace is that it is always a joint effort between God and mankind. We must first always invite and receive God's Spirit into our hearts and be submissive in our hearts to Him, for Him to work His Spirit of Grace in us. For example, we must humble ourselves and invite Christ into our hearts for Him to come into our hearts and perform the work of grace for our salvation. His response to our prayer is the work of grace to forgive us, to create in us new hearts, and to adopt us into His family. But, He will only come into our hearts after we willingly invite Him to come in; He does not come in just because He desires to come in because if He did, He would force Himself into everyone's heart. He wants us to desire Him enough to invite Him in.

When the Spirit of God in our hearts teaches us that we need to get rid of our temper or some other character problem, He will not make us change automatically. However, when we humble ourselves to His Word of correction, ask His forgiveness, invite to faith His Living Word of correction to come into our hearts, His Living Word, Christ, will perform the work of grace in us to help us overcome whatever the problem was that He identified to us. We grow in grace as He teaches us of our needs if we respond by inviting Him by faith into our hearts to perform the correction or to provide the strength of grace we need to make the correction. His action or work of grace in our heart is always after we invite Him to make the change or correction by our accepting His Words to faith. He will not force Himself into our hearts, and He will not force us to make the changes; we must be honestly willing and invite Him to come in and make the changes because of our love and commitment to Him. It is possible as we grow closer to the Lord after salvation for us to invite His Spirit into our hearts and allow Him to start making changes in our personality or beliefs but then we rebel or quench the Spirit of Grace which will stop the correction. Rejecting

His correcting Spirit of Grace is rejecting and blocking His Love from our hearts for that desired work of Grace, and our rejection is unbelief which gives satan the advantage in our lives during the time of our rebellion. The only way to correct this sin of rejection of His Grace in our hearts is to repent, ask God's forgiveness for the specific sin, and then receive His Words of correction, the Spirit of Grace, again into our hearts; this process of turning back to God and getting our hearts again in proper fellowship with God is what we call revival. Good, happy, gay worship and praise services are not revival services unless individuals repent, turn back their hearts to God from their previous sins of rejection, and accept again the work of Grace in their hearts for whatever they had previously rejected.

After the Spirit of Christ comes into our hearts, there are Scriptures that teach us to allow God to work in our hearts or to allow grace, the Spirit of Christ, to grow in our hearts. The Apostle Paul tells us how to prepare our hearts for God's work in *Colossians 3:16, "Let the word of Christ dwell in you richly in all wisdom; teaching and admonishing one another in psalms and hymns and spiritual songs, singing with grace in your hearts to the Lord."* We can "plow up and prepare the ground" of our hearts for the working of God's Spirit by making the effort to sing psalms, hymns, and spiritual songs or listen on the radio to them throughout the day to help keep our minds on the Lord. To help us with this throughout the week, I prefer a mixture of praise, worship, and old fashion hymns in our worship services. Along with the praise songs, we need some good hymns with words we can remember for singing through the week to help us keep our hearts and minds on Christ such as, "What a Friend We Have in Jesus," "Standing on the Promises," "Did You Think to Pray," etc. Some things in the Christian life are God's Will for all of us as Apostle Paul states in,

Ephesians 5:15-20.

(15) "See then that ye walk circumspectly, not as fools, but as wise,
(We should walk as children of God, not as fools who state there is no God, Psalms 14:1, but as the wise in Proverbs 11:30 who are sharing God's grace to reach the lost, non-Christians.)

(16) Redeeming the time, because the days are evil.
(By making our priority reaching out to lost people because our time is short.)

(17) Wherefore be ye not unwise, but understanding what the will of the Lord is. (This is the common will of God for all Christians.)

(18) And be not drunk with wine, wherein is excess; but be filled with the Spirit; (Only our sins keep us from continuing to be filled with the Spirit of God after we have first been filled.)

(19) Speaking to yourselves in psalms and hymns and spiritual songs, singing and making melody in your heart to the Lord;
(Our effort to welcome and prepare for the move of God's Spirit in us)

(20) Giving thanks always for all things unto God and the Father in the name of our Lord Jesus Christ." (Our love for God the Father, Jesus, and Christ, the Living Word, is reflected or shown by our gratefulness.)

In *2 Corinthians 12:9*, the Lord said to the Apostle Paul, *"...My grace is sufficient for thee: for my strength is made perfect in weakness."* The Lord was telling Paul that He would work His grace or love in Paul's heart that would carry him through all his persecutions. And the Lord did, for Paul was beaten, shipwrecked, bitten by a snake, stoned, and left for dead outside a city, and God delivered him from them all. However, Paul was so filled with the Love of God, or work of grace, that in *Acts 14:19 - 20* after Paul was stoned and left for dead, he was up the next morning on his way to preach and tell more people about Jesus, *"…and, having stoned Paul, drew him out of the city, supposing he had been dead. (20) Howbeit, as the disciples stood round about him, he rose up, and came unto the city: and the next day he departed with Barnabas to Derbe."* Those who stoned Paul actually thought he was dead or they would have kept stoning him, but even as bad a condition as he must have been in, God through His all-powerful Living Word, Christ, healed Paul and raised him up to be on his way again the next morning teaching and preaching the Love of God and Jesus. It is easy to see that the work of grace in Paul's heart was not just a philosophy, good feeling, or great goals for Paul to achieve in missionary work; the grace was another way of saying that the all-powerful, creative Living Word, the Spirit of Christ, was living and working in Paul's heart. As Christians, the same Spirit of Christ lives in our hearts and is the essence of the New Covenant that Jesus died to set into effect as stated in *Hebrews 9:16–17, "For where a testament is, there must also of necessity be the death of the testator. (17) For a testament is of force after men are dead: otherwise it is of no strength at all while the testator liveth."*

MERCY and GRACE

Clarification needs to be made of the true meanings and relationship of mercy and grace because of the confusion which is being taught by the seminaries, Bible schools, and ministers of every denomination in our Christian society. There are two main areas of concern: **First**, The error of teaching that there is grace in the Old Testament; and **Secondly**, The error of stating that grace is "God's unmerited favor." We must be very careful to use the correct words when describing God's movements in our lives in our teachings and testimonies to avoid adding confusion to the confusion that satan is already trying to create in our listeners.

Error of Grace in the Old Testament

If a person will take the Bible and a "Strong's Exhaustive Concordance of the Bible," or probably any other concordance, to study the word grace as it is used in the Old and New Testaments, it will be easy to find that every time the word grace is used in the Old Testament there was an error in translation, for the words translated should not have been grace, but most of the time favor, and in a couple cases, mercy. The Psalmist also states that the only relationships the godly people of the Old Testament had with God was through mercy and truth in *Psalms 25:10, "All the paths of the Lord are mercy and truth unto such as keep His covenant and His testimonies."* There were a lot of judgments and punishments for those who were not seeking to follow God, but for the people following God, they only had God's Love, mercy, to or on them which was accompanied by His favor, and God's Word, truth, to them for instruction and guidance. In *John 17:17, Jesus said, "...thy Word is truth."* Under the New Testament Covenant, we still have mercy, God's Love to or on us, and truth, God's Word to us, but we also have the work of grace, God's Love or God in us. When the word grace is used in the New Testament it is always associated with a Spiritual influence in the heart of mankind, and not the external mercy and favor of God's relationship with mankind in the Old Testament or with people today who have not received Christ into their hearts. The correct use of the word grace in the Bible is only in the New Testament, and grace is always the work of the Spirit of God, Spirit of Christ, Jesus, the Holy Spirit, or God working in the hearts of mankind. Grace is the word which explains how under the New Covenant we are "saved," by the work of God's Spirit, the Living Word Christ, when He enters our hearts, how He creates in us a new heart, adopts or engrafts us into the body of Christ or family of God, and then begins His residence or His Spirit begins living in our hearts, and we become new creatures, children of God. God's Word states in *John 1:17, "For the law was given by Moses, but grace and truth came by Jesus Christ."* Grace includes all of the above creative work of God's Spirit in our hearts and probably much more that we do not understand. Only Jesus had the Living Word, Christ, the all-powerful creative arm of God in His heart before the Day of Pentecost in *Acts Chapter 2*. Grace is always God working in our hearts; mercy and favor is always God working outside our hearts toward or on us.

Error of Calling Grace, "God's Unmerited Favor."

I cannot stress in written words the seriousness of how the devil has used the expression that "grace is 'God's unmerited favor," to degrade God's Loving image, confuse the Christian society and leave lost people without a clue as to how to obtain the saving grace for salvation. Christian ministers across our nation with smug looks and boastful voices will shout in pulpits, radio programs and television messages this upcoming weekend, *"Awww, God's grace! God's unmerited favor!"* and wait for live audiences to shout back, *"Amen! Amen!"* Then they will proceed to tell about God sparing someone's life in a fall, or car wreck, or a gun that failed to fire or thousands of other miracles which are not in our hearts and are due to the mercy of God in our lives, not grace. Only in about every fifteen to twenty messages on radio or television about grace will ministers even mention the changed heart or how we go about receiving the changed heart. Most of our ministers when talking about grace use examples of God's great mercy because they do not have a clear understanding of mercy and grace.

Mercy and favor normally went hand-in-hand in the Old Testament because as people sought to serve God, He was pleased with them because of their effort to respect and obey His Word. He would then manifest His love and blessings in special ways above their needs and they would call it His favor to them. The Scriptures state several times in the Old and New Testaments of the Bible that God is not a respecter of persons, and the Scripture states in *James 2:9, "But if ye have respect to persons, ye commit sin,..."* Since God does not have respect of persons, in the Old Testament His apparent consistent blessings and favor to one person above others came as a result of the person's respect of God by seeking to accept and obey God's Word because in *Psalms 138:2* the Scripture states that God has magnified His Word above all His names, *"I will worship toward thy holy temple, and praise thy name for thy lovingkindness and for thy truth: for thou hast magnified thy Word above all thy name."* His lovingkindness was His mercy to them and His truth was His Word.

Many times God intervenes through mercy to bless or show favor even when we are not in "Pleasing fellowship with Him," and this is called, *"God's unmerited favor;"* such as, when God stopped the angel from destroying the Israelites in *1 Chronicles 21:14-15, "So the Lord sent pestilence upon Israel: and there fell of Israel seventy thousand men. (15) And God sent an angel unto Jerusalem to destroy it: and as he was destroying, the Lord beheld, and He repented Him of the evil, and said to the angel that destroyed, 'It is enough, stay now thine hand...'"* Since these people were not in God's favor, this intervention by God through His mercy to stop the angel was "unmerited favor (through mercy), such as, in *Romans 2:4* where the Apostle Paul states that God blesses sinners to draw them to repentance. Both examples would be *"God's unmerited favor, mercy,"* to the Israelites by stopping the angel from killing more of them and by blessing unrepentant rebellious sinners, which would also include carnal Christians. The great "unmerited favor, mercy" of God was then and still is today, His mercy to unrepentant people, Christians and non-Christians, but not His Spirit in them producing a work of grace! God's blessings in both cases above are external to the hearts of the unrepentant people, but through His "unmerited favor" of His mercy today, He is trying to draw the unrepentant people into repenting and inviting His Spirit of Grace into their hearts. *"God's unmerited favor" is great, but it is not grace!* If it were not for "God's unmerited favor" when we were in the world as unrepentant sinners, the devil would have destroyed us before we would have been able to turn to God for salvation, *Ephesians 2:1-5, "And you hath He quickened, who were dead in trespasses and sins; (2) Wherein in time past ye walked according to the course of this world, according to the prince of the power of the air, the spirit that now worketh in the children of disobedience: (3) Among whom also we all had our conversation in times past in the lusts of our flesh, fulfilling the desires of the flesh and of the mind; and were by nature the children of wrath, even as others. (4) But God, who is rich in mercy, for His great love wherewith He loved us, (5) Even when we were dead in sins, hath quickened us together with Christ, (by grace ye are saved;)"* Jesus states in *John 10:10, "The thief cometh not, but for to steal, and to kill, and to destroy: I am come that they might have life, and that they might have it more abundantly."* God's great "unmerited favor, mercy," to us during our years of sin is the only means by which we were able to survive the devil's attacks and eventually be able to turn to the Lord for His saving grace. During the more than 20 years that I thought I was a Christian and wasn't, I came within seconds of being killed several times when something I thought was "weird" or unnatural happened to spare me. I was not sure then but thought it might have been God at times when I would reflect on the happenings, but now I know it was "God's great unmerited favor, mercy" to me. Even today when I think of those circumstances in my life when God stepped in through His mercy and spared me, I wonder why so many young people and, especially, young parents with children to raise are not spared from some of the terrible circumstances I see and read in the news like He spared me. But then I remember that God's mercy is not predictable or understandable from our view point because God intervenes as He chooses, *Romans 9:18, "Therefore hath He mercy on whom He will have mercy..."* Grace is always predictable because God will always back up His Living Word that we accept and receive into our hearts to produce in us the work of grace. Grace is always God working in our hearts at our request; mercy and favor is always God working outside our hearts toward or on us at His choice.

God's "unmerited favor, mercy" is discussed above when God in His mercy decided to stop His angel from killing all of the Israelites in *1 Chronicles 21:14-15* and "unmerited favor" is shown again in *Romans 2:4* where the Apostle Paul states that God blesses unrepentant sinners to draw them to repentance. Favor was the characteristic of God's good feeling toward the people when He responded in mercy to the Old Testament peoples' honest efforts to seek Him and follow His Will. Favor could not describe or be a defining word for grace because grace is always the "double sealed" promised response of God in *Hebrews 6:17* to all who will accept and receive His Word into their hearts to faith to produce the work of grace in their hearts. "Unmerited favor" given to the Israelites in *1 Chronicles 21* is certainly not how God decides who will or will not receive grace. In reality, we do not merit any of God's love -

mercy, grace, compassion, charity, or any other manifestation of God's love, it is only through Jesus that we are made acceptable to God and that is from a free-will choice of ours to accept and receive God's Word, Christ, into our hearts for salvation.

As great as "God's unmerited favor, mercy," is when we need Him, Grace is not randomly given out by God, as is His "unmerited favor;" grace is not a sporadic response of God, as is His "unmerited favor;" grace is not unpredictable or unrepeatable as is God's "unmerited mercy favor." Grace is predictable, repeatable, and one of the most dependable, loving acts of an all Loving God who will forgive sinners and then even engraft them into His family with new hearts the instant they respond in faith to His Living Word! I know every time, without any doubt, when I share the pure gospel message that anyone who responds positively by humbling themselves, asking God's forgiveness, and inviting His Spirit into their hearts ---that God will hear, forgive their sins, and put His Living Word, Christ, into their hearts to perform the work of grace to change their being into a new creature and a child of God. God's same predictable, repeatable response of grace to people who call out to Him can be predicted and depended on to happen every time, anytime, everyday, any person, every color, any nationality. I can predict with 100% assurance that God will continue to respond and make the same great changes in the hearts of all who in the future responds positively to His Love, and these same marvelous changes will continue to be repeated throughout the future over and over in every person's heart that turns to the Lord and asks for forgiveness! Grace is not God's random, unpredictable, unrepeatable "unmerited favor!"

The devil has caused Christians to choose the most random, sporadic, unpredictable, unrepeatable act of God, "God's unmerited favor, mercy)," to the Israelites and unrepentant sinners to represent grace which is the most dependable, predictable, repeatable act of God's greatest manifestation of Love toward mankind since the creation. Jesus' life is the foundation leading to our receiving grace, the work of the Spirit of Christ in our hearts, and the devil wants to degrade Jesus and His efforts for us with a lie which will create as much confusion as possible when Christians try to share the great love of God and beauty of grace to the lost and dying world. The process of establishing the New Covenant grace, God's Spirit working in our hearts, results from Jesus' suffering the perfect walk of faith, Jesus' suffering the seven sprinklings of His blood on the cross, Jesus' death, Jesus' burial, and Jesus' resurrection. The grace we receive because of Jesus' great suffering creates in us a new heart and engrafts us into the family of God as joint heirs with Jesus, the devils' main enemy. The devil wants to degrade grace in any way he can because grace in the hearts of mankind is the crowning fulfillment of Jesus' complete life of suffering for mankind. As great as "God's unmerited favor, mercy" was to the Israelites whose physical lives were spared in the story above, and how great "God's unmerited favor" is even today toward unrepentant sinners, (for we all have many times needed His "unmerited favor, mercy,") to call grace "God's unmerited favor" is totally 100% incorrect; an error and a lie, and is speaking despite against the Spirit of Christ or Grace! We can not speak an untruth, a lie, and glorify God just because it emotionally sounds good, and we can not build truth on an error in our messages. We can not build the truth in a message of grace that starts out with the lie of the devil to degrade Jesus and grace by calling grace "God's unmerited favor." To continue to use "God's unmerited favor" to describe or define grace would be willfully speaking disrespect and despite unto the life and suffering of Jesus and to God who loved us so much that He forgave our sins and engrafted us into His family through His great Spirit of Grace, Christ, in our hearts.

Grace always instantly follows our faith which comes from our free-will choice to accept into our hearts and obey God's Word He has revealed to us. Grace follows faith because when God reveals something to us through His Spirit, the Living Word, and we accept His Living Word to faith into our hearts, the Living Word coming into our hearts then becomes the Spirit of Grace to perform the action in us that God spoke to us and that we accepted into our hearts to faith. We grow in faith and grace every time we through our faith accept and receive God's Words into our hearts. When His Words of faith, Christ, enters our hearts, He then becomes the Spirit of Grace to produce a work of grace in us, and this is the great new relationship between God and mankind. The devil will do anything to confuse, distort, cover-up, degrade, or make light of grace, the work of God's Spirit in us, because when a sinner sees the wonderful works of grace in a person's life, the sinners will want the same work of grace in their hearts and life, *Revelation 12:11, "And they overcame him (the devil) by the blood of the Lamb, and by the word of their testimony; and they loved not their lives unto the death."* The Spirit of Grace performs the greatest work of God's Love to mankind, and each of us should make a commitment right now to never, never, never speak those words of disrespect again by incorrectly calling the Spirit of Grace "God's unmerited favor."

Even as great as "God's unmerited favor" is in our lives, we should show our love and respect for God, Jesus, and the Living Word, Holy Spirit, along with our concern for our listeners' souls that we will all commit to speak the words of grace and mercy correctly from this day forth. Lost people need to know clearly that grace in them can only happen, take place or exist, in them as a result of their personal choice to accept God's Words of salvation by faith into their hearts as shown in *Hebrews 4:2, "For unto us was the gospel preached, as well as unto them: but the Word preached did not profit them, not being mixed with faith in them that heard it."* The only way God's Word will profit any of us is by our acceptance and obedience to His Words in our hearts. So, when we speak of grace, we must tell about the great changes created in mankind's hearts; when we speak of mercy, we tell about God's great mercy and favor to obedient people and God's great mercy and "unmerited favor" to the disobedient people, but keep them separate and clear for many of our listeners are making eternal decisions based on our testimonies and teachings.

CHARITY

Charity is a New Testament word since it is a work of grace, God's Spirit in a Christian's heart, which is shared to edify, build others up in the Lord, whether the receiving person is a Christian or not. Because grace is a work of God's Spirit in a person's heart, only we Christians can perform acts of Biblical charity. Anyone can perform kind or good deeds toward others whether they are Christians or not, and in our society it would be called charity. But charity in the Scriptures is always associated with the work of grace in Christians' hearts which results in a sharing of that work of grace with others, or simply put, just *God working His Spirit through us Christians to others.* Charity is not referred to in the Old Testament because the grace of the Old Testament should have been translated "mercy" or "favor," for God did not work in the hearts of His Old Testament people because they only had mercy and truth. Therefore, grace and charity are both New Testament words which did not exist in the Old Testament period. Charity has been removed from all of the main new versions or copies of the Bible. *Edification,* a word very closely related to charity which means, *"to build up in the Lord,"* has been removed and replaced by "build up" in the new versions in about half of the times that it is used with charity in the King James Version (KJV) or Catholic versions. I challenge you to read in your Bible all of the Scriptures I copy in the following text to see how the verses read in whatever version of the Bible you commonly use. Also, a very good study would be to buy a concordance, and a copy of the KJV and read all of the verses which include the words charity or any form of the word, edify, to compare the verse meanings between the KJV and your newer version. You will find that the verses have very different meanings in the versions which have removed or replaced the words charity and edify. For example: "To edify," means to build up a person in the Lord, not to just "build up a person" which is used by the new versions. I can cause you to feel good or be "built up" by complementing you on your new car, pretty clothes, new hairdo, etc., but to "build up in the Lord" or to edify, I would need to show or speak my appreciation to you for your dedication in teaching a Bible class, being patient, praying with me about a concern of mine, etc. A lot of meaning and clarity is removed from Scriptures when charity and edification are replaced by "love" and "build up." Charity and edification are related in *1 Corinthians 8:1,* which states that "...*Charity edifieth."* In newer versions, the verse would say something like, "love builds up," which is true, but it does not show the beauty of God working His Spirit of Grace in and through one of His special, submitted, responsive people who then puts other things in his life aside to go and be a part of working with God to build up the other person in God's Living Word, Christ. True charity which is the work of God's grace in Christians' hearts and through their hearts to other people always edifies, "builds others up in the Lord," if the receiving people accept the love of the act of charity. The two commandments Jesus gave are to "love God with all your being" and to "love thy neighbor as thyself." Therefore, charity includes and fulfills both commandments as the Apostle Paul states in *1 Timothy 1:5, "Now the end of the commandment is charity out of a pure heart, and of a good conscience, and of faith unfeigned."*

When we take a detailed look at what charity includes, like we did before with grace, the beauty of the word and why it should still be used in the Scriptures will be seen. The first step in an act of charity starts with God wanting to work through one or more of His people to someone else in need, whether the need is physical, emotional or Spiritual. God must somehow speak to whomever He selects about what He wants them to do, and in making His selection the person must be one of His committed, available and responsive people. Many of God's people have turned Him down so many times when He asked them to serve or help others that He rarely asks them anymore. The person God chooses must be in an attitude that when God speaks he will hear God's Words, recognize the message as God's Words, and then choose to receive God's Words for the situation to faith into his heart. When the Words of Faith, or the Living Words, Christ, enter the person's heart, Christ begins the work of grace in the person's heart to prepare the person for whatever the action of charity will be. While the person is in the preparation stage of Christ working in his heart and preparing his heart, he will be walking-by-faith to the Words of Faith from God that he heard and received into his heart. The person must continue to stay submitted to God's Words, Christ, in his heart during the preparation, and when the proper opportunity arrives he must then perform the action of charity by continuing to walk-by-faith and speak the message or do whatever the Lord has asked of him, whether it be by word or deed. He must perform or deliver the action of charity which God desired of him by walking-by-faith, acceptance and obedience to God's Words, and with grace from his heart as carefully as possible with the correct attitude and as faithfully as possible to not change the message to the other person, and be as an ambassador who is delivering a message from the King, Christ Jesus. When the act of charity is completed, the person has then shared the same Love of God in his heart with the other person; therefore, charity has fulfilled God's law to "Love God and Love your neighbor as yourself," as again stated in *1 Timothy 1:5, "The end of the commandment is charity, out of a pure heart, and of a good conscience, and of faith unfeigned."* The Christian has submitted his heart to God (pure heart), has a good conscience (knows his motivation is pure and honest), and of unfeigned faith (knows God has spoken to him and he has received God's Words into his heart to faith), and now he performs with God the act of charity to the other person by delivering or performing the action of God's request. These specific actions required by God working in union with His Spirit in man to produce an act of charity shows the beauty of the word charity which is not reflected by just saying love. The person receiving the message will be receiving an act of God's mercy through charity, God and one or more of His people, instead of mercy directly straight from God to the individual. The person delivering the message will be performing an act of grace from his heart through charity and/or mercy to the other person. If the person who received the message does not immediately recognize the message as being from God, he should seek the Lord for his personal confirmation of the message. Once the message is confirmed as being from God, the person will have to make the choice to either receive the message to faith in his heart for edification by the work of grace, or reject the message to unbelief which will give satan the advantage in his life.   What a choice! It seems that all would accept, but many turn God down. The only way the work of charity will produce edification in the receiving person or people is if they receive the message into their hearts to faith.

The Apostle Paul instructs in *1 Corinthians 16:14, "Let all your things be done with charity."* We must let all our actions be done by charity, God's Spirit of Grace in and through our submissive hearts to others by our words or deeds. The Apostle Paul wanted his whole life to be used for God as an example to draw others to Christ. He states in *Colossians 3:14,* after discussing several great characteristics which we all as Christians should have, *"And above all these things put on charity, which is the bond of perfectness."* Putting on charity would be sharing Christ's grace in and from our hearts to others who are in return sharing God's grace from their hearts to us. If all of us Christians in our everyday lives were sharing Christ's love, grace, from our hearts to each other, we would be bonded together so tightly in true unity that the world would see our love, and the devil would not be able break us apart with picky, petty or prideful differences. With Christians joined in the true unity of grace and charity in our hearts to each other, even non-Christians would see the remarkable blessings of God so clearly on us and want to be a part of God's family, too. It sounds like a dream, but we must try to achieve this unity because only God's Pure Living Word, Christ, can bring us together through His work of grace in our hearts for us to ever reach the bond of charity that will change us and our society!

In *John 14:15*, Jesus said, *"If ye love me, keep my command-ments."* Obeying God's commandments is an evidence of loving God. Also in *1 John 5:2–3* the Scripture states, *"By this we know that we love the children of God, when we love God, and keep His commandments. (3)For this is the love of God, that we keep His commandments: and His commandments are not grievous."* When we obey God's commandments for personal daily activity, we are then loving God and His children through charity in the greatest manner possible. One of the ways that our learning to love God and share His Love in charity to others will change our society is that they will see the blessings in our lives increase as we start getting a lot more personal prayers answered for our families, friends, church and business acquaintances, and our nation. The Scriptures *state in 1 John 3:21-23, "Beloved, if our heart condemn us not, then have we confidence toward God. (22) And whatsoever we ask, we receive of Him; because we keep His commandments, and do those things that are pleasing in His sight. (23) And this is His commandment, 'That we should believe on the name of His Son Jesus Christ, and love one another,' as He gave us commandment."* If we are loving God and sharing in charity with others, we certainly will have a pure heart or it would not be true charity, and we would not be asking for "crazy" things, but for the needs of our family, friends, and others. If we are performing acts of charity, then God is working in and with us so that He will certainly be pleased with us, and we would also be receiving many more answers to our personal prayers. Our nation could be changed if Christians would seek the Lord with all their hearts for His Pure Word and then begin to share His Word and blessings through charity as priests to those people we meet in our daily world. The blessings of God would begin flowing so greatly that everyone would see and know it was God and not just made up testimonies. The joy of God working in the Christian society would greatly increase and continue to grow so that it would be uncontainable and undeniable! What an outpouring of His Spirit would be taking place! It is what most Christians have been looking and praying would soon happen, but it will only come after the Christian community first makes some honest changes from these terrible false teachings in our Christian society, for God is ready anytime if we will humble ourselves and make the changes!

Sometimes when we obey God, others will not receive what we say or do in a positive manner, but they did not receive the prophets, Jesus, or the disciples either. We must be sure it is God instructing us to say or do whatever we confess and do. We must take the time to seek the Lord to make sure of His Word to us, or we will ruin our testimony or witness to those around us if we claim that God told us to do things and there is never evidence of God backing up what we say He has told us. God will only back up His Pure Word, not just things we make up, even if they seem good. *Good is not necessarily God, but God is always good!*

Gifts of the Spirit

The operation of the gifts of the Spirit is a work of charity: God working in and through His children to edification by ministering to another's needs. This is stated in *1 Corinthians 12:7, "But the manifestation of the Spirit is given to every man to profit withal."* Charity is God manifesting gifts of His Spirit in and through His children for the common edification of all and the specific needs of individuals present. The Apostle Paul states that Prophecy, speaking God's Living Word, edifieth , but we know it only edifies if hearers receive the Prophecy Word by faith into their hearts, *"But he that prophesieth speaketh unto men to edification, and exhortation, and comfort," 1 Corinthians 14:3.* And in *1 Corinthians 14:4* the Scripture states, *"He that speaketh in an unknown tongue edifieth himself; but he that prophesieth edifieth the church [Body of Christ]."* It is not selfish or "bad" in any way for those of us who are "down" to speak in tongues to get edified or built back up in the Lord. The Lord gave the gift! How could it be "bad" or selfish in any way for someone to use the gift from God for the purpose God gives the gift? The Apostle Paul was alone many days and nights on some of his missionary trips, and because He suffered much to share God's Word he probably needed a lot of edification, to be built up in the Lord, many times on his long, lonely trips. Paul states in *1 Corinthians 14:18, "I thank my God, I speak with tongues more than ye all. . . ."* He did not mind at all confessing to others that he used the gift of tongues for his personal edification, and we should appreciate the fact that he did use the gift of tongues for if he had not used the gift of tongues for edification he might not have made it through all of his sufferings to provide us with his teachings in the New Testament. The Scripture, written by the Apostle Paul, states in *Ephesians 4:11–12, "And He gave some, apostles; and some, prophets; and some, evangelists; and some, pastors and teachers; (12) For the perfecting of the saints, for the work of the ministry, for the edifying of the body of Christ."* The Scripture states in *1 Corinthians 14:26, ". . . Let all things be done unto edifying."* And in *Romans 14:19, "Let us therefore follow after the things which make for peace, and things wherewith one may edify another."* Charity could be summed up by saying: let God work in and through your heart as He works with you that others may be edified and built up in the Lord. Edification for all involved is the end result of charity unless those to whom God is working toward rejects the act of charity, the love of God manifested to them.

When the Apostle Paul was discussing the gifts of the Spirit in *1 Corinthians 12*, he knew that people could obey God to faith and go forth attempting to serve God with the wrong attitude while grumbling and griping which is faith without love. So in the middle of his discussion of ministering the gifts to others, Paul stopped and said there is a "more excellent way." Obey God's Word and let your faith work with God by His love, or allow the His Spirit to work in your heart and then be channeled through you to others in a work of charity. These expressions are saying the same thing in different viewpoints. The end result is that we allow God to work with us or we choose to work with Him, to edify others, whether we say it is "faith that worketh by love" or through an act of charity. I have included my comments with each verse as the Apostle Paul explains the "more excellent way" in *1 Corinthians 13:1-8 and 13,*

(1) "Though I speak with the tongues of men and of angels, and have not charity [God working in his heart and through him to others], *I am become as sounding brass, or a tinkling cymbal* [Because doing the work by himself without God would be useless].

(2) And though I have the gift of prophecy, and understand all mysteries, and all knowledge; and though I have all faith [Acceptance and obedience to God's Word] *so that I could remove mountains, and have not charity* [Does not have God working in his heart and through him to others], *I am nothing.*

(3) And though I bestow all my goods to feed the poor, and though I give my body to be burned and have not charity [Does not have God working in his heart and through him to do these things], *it profiteth me nothing* [Because he would doing it without God].

(4) Charity suffereth long, and is kind; charity envieth not; charity vaunteth not itself, is not puffed up [If God were working in his heart to minister to someone, he would be long suffering and kind to the person. Paul could not envy someone if God were working in his heart and through him to minister to that person. Paul would not build himself up to someone or be puffed up if he were trying to share Christ with the person for salvation. He would be very careful not to offend the person in any way, since an offense from him might keep the person from accepting Christ as his Lord and Savior.]

(5) Doth not behave itself unseemly, seeketh not her own, is not easily provoked, thinketh no evil [Paul certainly would be careful of his actions if he were witnessing to others about Christ. He would not seek his own elevation, get mad or upset, or think evil of people that God was working in Paul's heart and ministering through him to lead to Christ. He would not try to steal something on the way out of their houses, lie to them or consider doing any wrong against them. He knew he could not do these things if it were truly God

working in him and through him to another person which would be the true work of charity. If any of these things existed in Paul's heart, then God would not be working in him or with him, and he knew it would not be a work of charity.]

(6) Rejoiceth not in iniquity, but rejoiceth in the truth. [Paul cannot rejoice in iniquity, sin, and have his heart submitted to God working in and through him to others. He cannot rejoice in dirty jokes, dirty movies, talk shows, dirty actions, transgressions of the law, lying, cheating, stealing, prejudices, or any other evil thoughts or actions and then claim to be operating in charity, which is God working in his heart and through him to others.]

(7) Beareth all things, believeth all things. Hopeth all things, endureth all things. [No comments.]

(8) Charity never faileth. [Charity never faileth because if God is asking Paul or us to go minister to someone's needs, and if we are the cleansed vessel for Him to work through, then He will work in us and through us to the other person and meet his need. It will not be us meeting the other person's need, but it will be God meeting the other person's need, and He never fails. That is why it is so important that we stay submitted and set apart holy for His use. He will work through us to meet others' needs only if we allow Him to go with us in a cleansed vessel.]

(13) And now abideth faith [Acceptance and obedience to God's Word], *hope* [The desired outcome based on our "faith"], *charity* [Allowing God to work in our hearts and through us to others], *these three; but the greatest of these is charity."*

Our faith does not necessarily include love, for we can obey God while griping and complaining. Our hope, our desired outcome, is based on our desires that may not always be in the correct direction. However, charity always includes true faith, our acceptance and obedience to God's Word with love, and the corresponding correct hope, since God has told us what He wants us to do, and then God performs His work of charity in and through us. If we love God enough to allow Him to work His love in our hearts through our obedience to faith, God will minister His gifts of the His Spirit to others' needs which will result in the hope or desired outcome always being fulfilled because Love never fails! The true work of charity will result in God's moving without hindrance through us to others like water flowing freely through a hose. Jesus said in *John 7:38, "He that believeth on me, as the Scripture hath said, out of his belly shall flow rivers of living water,"* and the Scripture states in *Proverbs 11:30, "The fruit of the righteous is a tree of life; and he that winneth souls is wise."*

Sin

Sin does not seem to fit into a discussion of God's love, grace, in and through His children's hearts performing acts of charity to mankind, but I think you will see that this is the best time to explain truly what sin is and to understand how it hurts God, ourselves, and all of those around us. One of the two main modern explanations or definitions of sin is called *missing-the-mark*. Sin is not missing-the-mark! Missing-the-mark implies we practiced and tried the best we could to shoot and hit the bull-eye of a target, but since we are all human and none of us are perfect, we just could not hit the bulls-eye---we missed-the-mark! That's not sin! If we do the best we can for God, He will be pleased and will help us do better. The *second most used explanation of sin is breaking laws that tell us not to murder, rob, or rape, and these are not SIN either; they are acts of sin.* Jesus taught in the Sermon on the Mount in Matthew Chapters 5, 6 and 7 and in many other places that sin is the break of fellowship of the heart with God. When the fellowship or union of our heart with God's Spirit is broken, we have sinned. We will perform many evil acts of sin, but sin is only the blocking of God's love, His Living Word, Christ, from entering into our heart for whatever the situation God is speaking to us. Murder only takes place after we have blocked God's love in our heart for someone and then we allowed hate to grow and overflow to the person in an act of sin which could be murder or many other things. For Christians, all acts of sin, robbery, rape, idol worship, and adultery only take place after we break God's flow of love into our hearts, and instead allow lusts, hate, greed and pride to come into our hearts again. We Christians never lose all of God's Living Word in us, but just like we can grow in grace by receiving more of God's Word in us, we can also lose grace by rejecting God's Word which we had previously received to faith and grace. A simple example of a Christian sin that does not mean we have lost our salvation is discussed in *2 Corinthians 2:10-11* which says that we must forgive others lest we give satan the advantage in our lives. We know it is God's Will for us to forgive others; therefore, when we willfully reject God's Word for us to forgive others and the work of grace in our hearts for someone because we decide to not forgive them, we are breaking our proper fellowship and union with God and blocking His Love, the work of grace into our hearts and through us to the other person. We have cut or stopped the flow of God's Love in and through us to the other person and –*that is SIN!*

Non-Christians do not have the Spirit of Christ in their hearts and must live by some moral code they hopefully have been taught which will keep them from performing the acts of sin. Even though non-Christians can perform a lot of terrible, evil, deeds or acts of sin, their only SIN is the separation of their heart from God, and that is no different than we all were before accepting Christ. The non-Christian's heart is totally void of God, the Spirit of Christ or any other name you might call God because we are all born with a heart empty of God's Spirit, or in total Spiritual separation from God, or we are born in total **SIN**! We do not sin against people. We obviously can commit terrible acts of torture and destruction to others, but the sin is when we in our hearts break the flow of God's Love. When we willfully break our union with God and the flow of His Love to and in our hearts, as mentioned above, we have given the devil advantage and control in our lives. The devil knows we are out of fellowship with God so he will then try to lead us into all kinds of evil activity which might result in many evil acts against others because of our sin.

We have just discussed charity and shown that charity is the name given for the work of God's love in and through a Christian's heart that is then shared to edify, build others up in the Lord. Sin for Christians is first when we break the flow of God's love to us personally from coming into our hearts for our personal edification, and then secondly when we break the flow of God's love in and through our hearts to others that God wants us to share His Love with in acts of charity. First, God may be teaching us that we need to change something in our lives; such as, our temper, bad language, drinking, smoking, etc. When we recognize God speaking to us and that He wants us to make a personal change, if we refuse to accept His Word of correction to faith in our hearts, then we have also refused the work of grace needed in our hearts to help us make His desired change in us, and that is sin. We have blocked God's love from our hearts for that situation and we have sinned! God hurts because we will not let Him make us who He wants us to be for the future use He has for us. We hurt because we have refused to receive His love, and we will be in unbelief and out of fellowship with God during this time of our rejection. All of those around us will miss blessings because we will never become the people God wants us to be to help edify them, and our neighbors will not even know they are missing blessings because we are out of fellowship with God. Also, many of our prayers for our loved ones, friends, businesses, and our country will go unanswered while we are out of fellowship with God by willfully choosing to reject His love in our hearts for our correction, and also anytime we willfully reject God's Word we are giving satan the advantage in our lives. The second way Christians sin is as discussed above when God is trying to use us to share His love through us with someone as an act of charity, but we have unforgiveness or other bad feelings for that person. We will be sinning because we will be blocking God's Love from entering into our hearts and through our hearts to perform an act of charity to that person. God hurts because after all His Love for us, and all His forgiveness to us, we still do not love Him enough to receive His love in our hearts for the person for whom we are refusing to forgive. The Scriptures state in *Ephesians 4:32, "And be ye kind one to another, tenderhearted, forgiving one another, even as God for Christ's sake hath forgiven you."* We hurt because we cannot receive the extra love God wants to put in our hearts for the other person we have chosen not to forgive. When we reject any of God's Word to unbelief and are out of fellowship with God, the devil has advantage in our lives as discussed above. During this time, the devil will bring as much evil, curses, and destruction as he can sneak into our lives while we delay repenting and turning back to ask God's forgiveness. God cannot forgive us though unless we have prepared our hearts to forgive the other person because we hold the switch to forgiveness; we chose to forgive, and God will forgive us; while we are refusing to forgive, we have switched God off and He cannot forgive us because we have pushed Him away by our unforgiveness to the other person. The evidence of sin and the devil having been given control in Christians can be seen if we first look at the curses in *Deuteronomy 28* and then compare those curses to what we see in the lives of Christians around us. God does not bring curses into our lives, and God does not allow curses when we are submitted to His control, and curses do not just happen, *Proverbs 26:2 says, "...So the curse causeless shall not come."* The only way Christians can receive the curses in *Deuteronomy 28* is to have willfully given satan control in their lives by rejecting some of God's Word. In most cases their rejection probably seemed to be unimportant at the time when they did it because it only resulted in little sinful acts like, "white lies," gossip, arguing, envying, lusting, prejudices, respect of persons, and other common every day sinful acts that are not often even visible to others around us. But these everyday occurrences as small as they seem to be are still sin, the rejection of God's Love in our hearts and through us for those situations, and they also give the devil the advantage in each of these situations. The greatest healthcare program any of us Christians could have is to get on our knees now and ask God's forgiveness for all of those years of giving satan the advantage in our lives through these "little" sins, and then start showing fear and respect for God's Word. Christians sin when we fail to let the grace of God grow in our hearts, or when we refuse to allow God to work His Grace through our hearts to others in an act of charity. In both cases we are refusing God's Love from our hearts which is refusing the work of grace for whatever the situation is that God is asking of us.

The ideal situation is for us to live filled with the Spirit of Christ, the Living Word in our hearts. Jesus is the only One who received and walked in the fullness of the Spirit continually. In *John 1:14* the Scripture states, *"And the Word was made flesh, and dwelt among us, (and we beheld His glory, the glory as of the only begotten of the Father,) full of grace and truth."* And the Scripture states in *John 3:34, "For He whom God hath sent speaketh the Words of God: for God giveth not the Spirit by measure unto Him."* We all grow in receiving the Spirit of Christ in our hearts as we receive more of God's Living Word, Christ. The Apostle Paul explains this truth in *Ephesians 4:7, "But unto every one of us is given grace according to the measure of the gift of Christ,"* for Christ is the Living Word. As we study and receive more of the Living Word, Christ, into our hearts, we are growing in faith and grace. Paul also states in *Ephesians 4:11-13, "And He gave some, apostles; and some, prophets; and some, evangelists; and some, pastors and teachers; (12) For the perfecting of the saints, for the work of the ministry; for the edifying (building up in the Lord) of the body of Christ: (13) Till we all come in the unity of the faith, and of the knowledge of the Son of God, unto a perfect man, unto the measure of the stature of the fullness of Christ."* Jesus came in the fullness of the Spirit of the Living Word working in His heart, grace, and in the fullness of God's spoken Word, truth. We each will grow in His Spirit and grace as we receive through our faith God's Living Word into our hearts to produce the work of grace for growth in us. Every time we hear God's Word we have the opportunity to grow in grace, to grow in Christ, and to grow in faith if we make the free-will choice to receive God's Word into our hearts to faith and grace. We have the total free-will choice. God will not make us accept His Word, and the devil cannot keep us from accepting God's Word or make us reject God's Word. Our growth in the Lord is totally based on our free-will choices and that is why it is so important to be praying, studying the Bible, and seeking opportunities to hear God's Rhema, the Living Word, Christ. We should each make our commitment right now to set aside time each day to pray and study God's Word. We can each grow in His Spirit, grace, and faith as much as we choose; there is no limit. *Choose Faith, God's Word, with Love, God's Spirit!*

SUMMARY

God is Love, is the same as saying the Holy Spirit is Love, the Spirit of Christ is Love, and God, regardless of what name we call Him, is Love. God says beside Him there is no other God; therefore, because God is Love, beside Him there is no other love. The words eros (sexual) and phileo (friendly) are not love. They are strong feelings of sexual desire or friendly attraction, but they are not love. Only God is Love. There are not three kinds of love. There is only one Love, and that is the one God. The words mercy, grace and charity are used to describe different works of God's manifested love to and in mankind.

Mercy: The Scriptures show mercy as the one-way love to others, which does not require any form of response. In most cases, any response at all is negative. For God to use us to share Him or mercy through us to others, we must keep our hearts clean of unforgiveness, prejudices, envy, etc. We then can become the channel of blessings for God to work through us to those around us. We must keep our channels free of sin to be used with the flow of God through us. Mercy is associated with God's positive favor when He is working in the lives of those who are trying to serve Him. God's "unmerited favor, mercy" is in the lives of unrepentant sinners who may be non-Christians who have not turned their hearts to God or Christians who have rejected some of God's Word. Both kinds of mercy favor have been used for many blessings in all of our lives.

Grace: Grace is the work of God, God's love, the Holy Spirit, or the Spirit of Christ, in our hearts. One characteristic of the work of grace is that it is a joint effort between God and man. We must open our hearts, invite God in, and then be submissive in our hearts to Him, for Him to work His Spirit of Grace in us. He will not force us to do His will or to be submissive to His Word. We have the free-will to make our choice which is to either choose to accept His Word to faith into our hearts to grace, or to reject His Word from entering our hearts which is unbelief. If we accept His Word of correction to faith in our hearts, His Word, Christ that we receive into our hearts by faith will become the work of grace to make the desired correction in our hearts. The first instant the Spirit of Christ comes into our hearts we are saved. For salvation, the instant we respond to God in faith and invite the Spirit of Christ to come into our hearts, God sends the Spirit of Christ into our hearts and then Christ, the Living Word, produces the saving work of grace to create our new heart and engraft us into the family of God. The instant the Spirit of Christ enters our hearts, we are children of God and "saved" from penalty of our sin debt.

The use of the word grace in the New Testament is always associated with the work of the Spirit of God, Spirit of Christ, Jesus, the Holy Spirit or God working in the hearts of mankind. The New Testament grace is God working in the heart, never outside the person. Grace was incorrectly used in the Old Testament when someone had found "favor" in the eyes of God or some other person, never associated with a work of the Spirit in the hearts of mankind. All of the references of grace in the Old Testament should have been translated "mercy" or "favor." *And again, never say that grace is "God's unmerited favor."* "Unmerited favor" is God's great mercy to unrepentant sinners prior to salvation and to Christians who have rejected some of God's Word to them after salvation. Always say that grace is the work of the Spirit of Christ in our hearts; first for salvation and to help us to become like Christ as we grow in our faith.

MERCY GRACE CHARITY
GOD'S LOVE TO MANKIND

Charity: Charity is a work of grace that overflows from a Christian or is shared to edify or build others up in the Lord. The two commandments Jesus gave us are to love God and to love our neighbors as ourselves. Therefore, charity includes and fulfills both commandments, because charity starts with God working in the heart of one or more Christians and then they allow God to work through them to share the same love of God through them to another person.

Gifts of the Spirit: The operation of the gifts of the Spirit is a work of charity: God working in and through His children as they together, God and man, jointly minister to others' needs. Edification, being built up in the Lord, is the end result of both charity and the operation of the Gifts of the Spirit as God reaches out through His people to others, unless the individuals to whom the love is directed rejects the love of God shared with them.

Sin: Sin is when we chose to break the flow of God's love into our hearts or through our hearts to others. Sin is not missing-the-mark! Sin is when we willfully reject God putting His love in our hearts for a particular situation or person. Sin hurts everyone: God, us, and everyone else. With sin blocking God's love from coming into our hearts, we will not become the people God wants us to be, and others will not receive the blessings that God wants to channel through us to them. While we are sinning, blocking God's Love into our hearts, we will be willfully giving satan the advantage of control in our lives and his only purpose is to destroy us.

Put your hand in the hand of the man – who loves you – Jesus!
God Bless You!

BOOKS BY THE AUTHOR

Richard A Hardin

Rhardin77@yahoo.com

See summaries of all books at:

"Choosing Faith with Love"

all books www.rahardin.com.

"God Loved Esau"

www.createspace.com/3448063

"Prayer Changes Things"

www.createspace.com/3453781

"Choose Faith and Grace"

www.createspace.com/3465162

"Mercy, Grace, Charity"

www.createspace.com/3482157

"Jesus"

www.createspace.com/3482215

WEEKLY RADIO
AND
INTERNET PROGRAM

Internet Radio Program

www.ktlr.com/

Click link: "Listen Online"

In the Oklahoma City Local Radio Area

KTLR – AM 890 and FM 94.1

Time: 9:30-10:30 A.M.

Central Standard Time

Weekly, Saturday morning.